Uphill
Both
WAYS

Sara "Dolly" Leighton

Gospel Advocate Company
Nashville, Tennessee

Also by Dolly Leighton

Shine Like Stars: A Study of Philippians

Published by Gospel Advocate Co.
1006 Elm Hill Pike, Nashville, TN 37210
http://www.gospeladvocate.com

ISBN-10: 0-89225-562-5
ISBN-13: 978-0-89225-562-7

Dedication
Dedicated to my brother, George L. ("Corky") Brian
who made straight paths for my feet to follow.

Special thanks to Dr. Peggy Barger who started me on this literary journey; Dr. Lori Barr who inspired me to move forward when I parked for a while; and David Stofel, Debra Wright, Janie Craun and Michelle Burke who checked for potholes and pitfalls in my path.

Table of CONTENTS

PHOTOS

1. The inside of L.L. Brian General Merchandise Store

2. Dolly sitting on the running board of her father's 1946 Dodge. Her brother, Corky, is sitting inside.

3. Dolly and Corky surrounded by Christmas gifts. Dolly received her annual Christmas doll and a pair of house shoes.

4. Dolly with her favorite doll

5. Dolly and her brother, Corky

6. Dolly's maternal grandmother, Laura Haggarty

7. Granny Haggarty and Aunt Dixie

8. The second grade class at Ethridge school taught by Miss Ruby O'Rear. Dolly is the first girl in the third row next to Miss Ruby.

9. The inside of historic Crockett Theater. Seats for the black residents of Lawrenceburg were at the rear of the balcony on the right.

10. Dolly making cornbread at the kitchen table. Cooking was a skill her mother deemed necessary for young ladies.

11. Dolly talks to her hens about laying more eggs. This photo was taken by Howard Cooper to go with a story about Dolly in the Nashville Tennessean Magazine Section written by Elmer Hinton.

12. Sims Ridge Church of Christ in 1955

13. Dolly posed, unhappily it seems, by the piano she used to practice.

Introduction

The familiar expression "uphill both ways" has become a metaphor for hard times. Every time the young child complains about school or the amount of homework expected, his ancient grandfather responds in a quivering voice, "What are you complaining about? Why, when I was your age, I had to walk 10 miles to school barefoot through the snow, uphill both ways."

Like you, I have faced some hard times – temptation, the death of loved ones, bullying and prejudice. Still, not every memory of these experiences is a bad one. While writing the stories from my childhood that introduce each chapter in this book, I enjoyed recapturing the viewpoint of my youth: my desires, my emotions and even my selfish thinking.

My life could have been much worse by the standards of the day (the late 1940s and '50s). My parents were not poor; we were a middle-class family unstressed by financial worries because my dad and mother were in their late 30s and had a well-established business by the time I came along. However, when compared with the overindulgence and easygoing discipline of today's children, my parents' frugality may horrify many readers. Let me assure you, I was unharmed in any way and am appreciative of my parents' strict child-rearing practices.

Did my husband and I bring up our sons in the same way? If you ask my adult children, they will probably say yes just to embarrass me –

they love to tell horror tales about having me as a mother. If you ask me, however, I will say in some ways, yes, in other ways, no. If we are wise, we take the good from our childhood and leave the not-so-good behind. The ability to recognize what was expedient and what was not comes only with the passage of time when we can look at our experiences more objectively and acknowledge the motivations we could not see as children. And although we learn from the mistakes of our parents, we must realize that they too were affected by their life experiences. For example, my parents' frugality came from living through the Great Depression and World War II.

My memories are uniquely mine, but I know that other women my age have similar experiences to recall from beneath the weight of years – experiences that would be profitable to share with those who are younger. The purpose of this book is exactly that: to encourage ladies to share their childhood experiences and to use my stories and theirs as stepping stones for an excursion into biblical principles.

The Preacher in Ecclesiastes says, "That which has been is what will be, that which is done is what will be done, and there is nothing new under the sun" (1:9). Later, Paul tells Titus, "Older women likewise … admonish the young women to love their husbands, to love their children" (Titus 2:3-4). Despite coming from a past that no longer exists, our old-time experiences teach lessons that are applicable to today's generation, especially young mothers trying to guide their children through the pitfalls and pressures of the present age. Much joy is to be found in sharing our lives, and what better way to teach than through "When I was your age … ." It matters not that our experiences are from "the olden days"; actually, it is the archaic nature of our stories that makes them so interesting to those who are younger. Despite the years that have transpired, women of today will recognize in themselves many of the same desires, emotions and thoughts we older counterparts felt when we were their age.

My hope is that in this study we may glean truths from our sepia-tinted memories and apply them to the digitized world of the modern generation. By reflecting on our childhood days, we can discover the commonality of our experiences and the biblical principles to apply to our lives. Ultimately, when we have "shod [our] feet with the preparation of the gospel of peace" (Ephesians 6:15), we can encourage each other during those times we feel like we have to walk uphill both ways.

How to Study This Book

Subjects not normally included in ladies study books are featured in the chapters that follow (i.e., superstition, animal care, attitudes toward death, bullying, prejudice). Although the chapters are arranged according to the chronological order of the "Barefoot With Dolly" stories, you may choose to study the subject matter in any order because each chapter stands alone.

Each chapter contains a "Barefoot With Dolly" section, which describes an event in my childhood. After that, the "Rest a Spell" section provides thoughtful questions to bring back your own memories to share with the class. The "Walking With the Master" section in each chapter provides biblical application for the memories you have just discussed. And finally, the "Shod With the Preparation of the Gospel" section provides material for discussing what you have learned and discovering how you can apply it to the world around you.

Chapter 1 *Picture*

Taming TEMPTATION

"No temptation has overtaken you except such as is common to man; and God is faithful, who will not allow you to be tempted beyond what you are able, but with the temptation will also make the way of escape, that you will be able to bear it."
(1 Corinthians 10:13)

Barefoot With Dolly

As a child, I was a victim of abuse – at least, that's what I thought at the time. Our house was on the south side of Ethridge, Tenn., away from the hubbub of the downtown area on the north side where my dad's general merchandise store was located. Here was where all the action took place. Old men with names like Rob, Wormy, Shep and Mose whittled cedar sticks with their pocket knives while gossiping about county politics and the latest community happenings. Children who lived nearby swung repeatedly around the metal posts supporting the tin roof overhead and chased each other amid the horse-drawn carriages of the local Amish parked along the concrete porch.

Inside Daddy's store was an array of every kind of goods anyone could need in our community. Oil lanterns, horseshoes, horse collars, and 100-pound sacks of flour were all for the Amish. Everyone could choose from electric stoves, water heaters, bathroom sets, septic tanks, nuts, bolts, screws, groceries, paint, shotgun shells, fishing gear, cow feed, well curbs, cement, salt blocks, gardening tools and grass seed. "You need it, we have it!" was the motto.

On cool summer evenings, my mother and I would walk the 10 blocks or so from our quieter side of town to the store to ride home with my dad in his '46 Dodge when he closed up for the evening. I was always eager to go. I knew what a treasure trove awaited me in the midst of all the less interesting goods. I craved, I relished, I drooled over these delicacies. First, icy cold bottles of Coca-Cola, NuGrape soda, Dr Pepper, and RC Cola were waiting in the refrigerated drink box that was strategically placed beside the screen door to tempt all who entered there. To the left were the Baby Ruth candy bars, GooGoo Clusters, Cracker Jacks, and Juicy Fruit chewing gum, all protected from sticky little fingers by a glass case in plain view of the clerk at the cash register. And beside the adding machine on the counter were the glass jars with their piles of lollipops, Dubble Bubble gum, and jawbreakers. It was a childhood heaven.

The problem – and this was how I was abused – was that I was never allowed to partake of these wonderful, tasty treats. No matter how much I begged, no matter if I had cried and thrown a temper tantrum (which I knew better than to do), the answer remained no. I was definitely the most deprived child in all of Ethridge; and to make matters worse, my dad had the keys to this emporium of delights that I was so emphatically denied.

Making the situation even more unfair was the fact that none of these wonderful items ever made it home. In all my years growing up, I never saw a Coca-Cola or candy bar in our house. Oh, I received a valentine box of chocolates from my dad once a year, but that was it. On the sly, I did have my regular sources for chewing gum, though. Three high school boys who walked up the hill past our house from the bus stop would occasionally bless me with just one piece of gum when they could afford it. I waited impatiently every afternoon on the front lawn in hopes of their generosity. My small successes, however, paled in comparison to the wonderful gooey feast I was denied at Dad's store.

When I was 4 years old, the PTA at the Ethridge Elementary School sponsored a talent show to make money for a new cafeteria and, hopefully, the first indoor bathrooms. My mother, being an active community leader, decided to help out by entering me in the contest. I was to sing a solo, accompanied by my brother, Corky, who was 9 years older and a fairly good pianist. My mother taught me the words to "A Tree in the Meadow," and my brother learned the accompaniment. We practiced for several weeks, perfecting our act until I knew every word by heart.

The night of the competition, I mounted the tall wooden stage in the school auditorium, and my brother sat at the upright piano on the floor below. I looked confidently out over the crowd assembled there and found my mother's face. She opened her mouth widely, a signal for me to do likewise because we had no microphone. Loudly and clearly, I sang out the words of the song. I made it through the entire song without a hitch and was awarded with applause and smiles. A 7-year-old who had performed on the radio sang after me. She stopped in the middle of her number and, looking at her mother, said, "What did you say, Mommy?" Other participants performed, and of course, it was all more or less entertaining to the local citizenry.

Imagine my surprise when the winners were announced and my name was not called for third or second, but for first place. The prize, donated by none other than L.L. Brian General Merchandise store, was presented to me. I was ecstatic, not because I had won, but because of what I had won – a big box filled with Baby Ruth candy bars. At last I would have my greatest desire fulfilled. At last I would get to eat all those goodies I had been denied.

Back home after the show, I sat down in the middle of the living room floor with my prize and munched and munched and munched. The fact that I broke out in a rash, as I did every February after Valentine's Day, and had to be painted all over with Calamine lotion to stop the itching was a small price to pay for my triumphant prize.

Rest a Spell

1. Most of us thought our parents were being cruel when they denied us something we really wanted. Share a similar experience, your reaction as a child, and how your perspective has changed now that you are older.
2. Do you think Dolly's parents were too strict in not allowing her to have the candy and colas in her dad's store? What was their motivation?
3. Why is the temptation of unhealthy eating so hard to control?

4. What have you learned about nutrition in recent years that was not common knowledge when you were growing up? Has this knowledge changed the way you prepare foods or eat?
5. What foods do you ban or limit in your home to improve family nutrition?
6. Should we reward children in our Bible classes with candy, gum or snack foods?
7. Does the removal of temptation work as a way to overcome temptation?

Walking With the Master

In one of my primary-school readers was the story of a boy who received a candy dog made of peppermint sticks. It was so cute that he wanted to keep it forever. He kept opening the wrapping to admire the little red and white dog and finally decided that eating just one leg wouldn't hurt. He closed the wrapping – only to return to eat another leg. He repeated his actions until he ate the other legs and then the tail. Finally, the whole candy dog disappeared. Temptation is like that. First we look, then we taste, then we taste again. Finally, it becomes a part of us.

To tempt is "to entice to do wrong by promise of pleasure or gain: allure to evil: seduce" ("Tempt," def. 1). Everything God created is good; temptation, however, subverts that good, making it evil through excess or misuse. Eating enough to maintain health is good (Matthew 15:32); gluttony is sin (Philippians 3:19). Loving ourselves is necessary for us to love others (Mark 12:31); narcissism and vainglory are sins (2 Timothy 3:2). Strong opposition to worldliness is expected of God's child (2 Timothy 4:2); uncontrolled anger is sin (Ephesians 4:26-27). Providing for one's family is commanded by God (1 Timothy 5:8); "keeping up with the Joneses" is sin (James 5:1-3). Physical love between a husband and wife is permitted in God's plan for the home (1 Corinthians 7:2-5); living together outside of marriage is fornication and sin (Colossians 3:5). Children are to be the result of a physical union within the context of marriage (Psalm 127:3-5); procreation outside of wedlock is sin (Matthew 5:27-28). Humility is a Christian virtue (Philippians 2:3); pride in one's humility is sin (Colossians 2:20-23). The list of opposites – good subverted to evil – is infinite.

Underlying all temptation is gratification of our egos. We often see ourselves as the center of the universe, and we demand to be in control of it. When Eve met the serpent in the Garden of Eden, the beauty and food value of the forbidden fruit were not the chief attributes that tempted Eve to taste it. In fact, these qualities were not pointed out by the serpent at all but were added extraneously by Eve herself. The real draw was to be all-knowing or as wise as God – in other words, to become God (Genesis 3:4-6). Eve saw the fruit as a source of power over her life, eliminating her need for God.

As with Eve in the beginning, Satan especially chooses this temptation because it provides the context for all other temptations. The delectable fruit of the modern age is humanism that purports to disenfranchise God and claim that man can control his own life. Many of us have absorbed this type of thinking unwittingly. For example, my schoolmates and I were asked by our English teachers to study and/or memorize the classic poem "Invictus" by William Ernest Henley that ends with these lines, "I am the master of my fate; I am the captain of my soul." Henley did not subscribe to organized religion and, during a long hospitalization, came to rely on his inner strength. "Invictus" was his humanist credo ("Henley").

This self-reliance, when taken a step further by modern humanists, becomes disbelief in any absolute authority or truth outside of one's own self. As Jeremiah warned Judah before their captivity: "Thus says the Lord, 'Cursed is the man who trusts in man And makes flesh his strength, Whose heart departs from the Lord' " (17:5). As in those ancient days, so today many people subscribe to this philosophy: if it feels good, do it.

The first step in guarding our lives against the devil's temptations is to make sure that we do not base our lives on humanistic beliefs. We must subject ourselves totally to God and His will. Paul warned the Colossians: "Beware lest anyone cheat you through philosophy and empty deceit, according to the tradition of men, according to the basic principles of the world, and not according to Christ" (2:8). And lest we question the existence of absolute authority, Paul adds that Christ is "the head of all principality and power" (v. 10).

Timothy received a similar message from his mentor: "O Timothy!

Guard what was committed to your trust, avoiding the profane and idle babblings and contradictions of what is falsely called knowledge" (1 Timothy 6:20). Finally, we must take to heart Paul's exhortation, "If anyone among you seems to be wise in this age, let him become a fool that he may become wise" (1 Corinthians 3:18). Once we accept that God is in control of our lives and that true wisdom comes from above (James 3:17), we will have a bulwark to protect us against the devil's assaults.

It is not God who tempts us. James warns, "Let no one say when he is tempted, 'I am tempted by God'; for God cannot be tempted by evil, nor does He Himself tempt anyone" (1:13). Rather, we must realize that Satan is the father of lies and the tempter of us all (John 8:44; Matthew 4:3). He lays out his emporium of delights, sometimes even in the presence of God where we least expect it and entices us with the "passing pleasures of sin" (Hebrews 11:25). Our temptations are very personal in nature; the devil finds our weakest point and attacks. He has no boundaries except those inherent in God's promise that He "is faithful, who will not allow [us] to be tempted beyond what [we] are able, but with the temptation will also make the way of escape, that [we] may be able to bear it" (1 Corinthians 10:13).

God provides us with two common-sense modes of escape: (1) we can remove ourselves from where the temptation is, or (2) we can remove the temptation from our vicinity. In other words, absence equals abstinence. If, for example, my weakness is alcoholic beverages, I can remove myself from the temptation by avoiding bars and nightclubs. On the other hand, if my boss gives me a bottle of champagne for Christmas, I can avoid taking it home with me, thus removing the temptation from my environs.

Most of the time, however, our only choice is to remove ourselves; the tempting situation cannot be eliminated. For instance, a person subject to road rage in traffic jams can only choose to remove herself from the situation. She can find an alternative method of commuting, leave earlier or later when the roads are clear, find employment close to home, or become an at-home worker. To remove all commuters and their vehicles from her present path is fantasy at its best.

In some situations, however, abstinence through absence proves to be an impossible answer. Some temptations require the more difficult solution of temperance. "Temperance" is best defined for the Bible student in the 1913 edition of *Webster's*: "Habitual moderation in regard to the indulgence of the natural appetites and passions; restrained or moderate indulgence." How easy this is to preach, how hard to practice. For instance, I have a problem with overeating. Unfortunately, I cannot abstain from food and live. Temperance is the key, but, oh, how hard it is to deny myself that extra helping of potatoes or that piece of pecan pie. Satan knows he has me on this one because I cannot choose perpetual fasting.

Although the synonym for "temperance" in the definition is "moderation," the key word is "habitual" because it determines the degree to which we practice moderation or self-control. The word "habitual" implies building, through long practice, a habit. Habits do not come easily. A basketball player practices shooting foul shots to improve her percentage of successful goals, but she never becomes perfect. Similarly, habits are never 100 percent perfect, but more often than not, with practice they work in our favor. The more we use the habit of moderation, the closer to perfection we can come.

Our willpower will be perfected or completed even more through the ultimate source of resistance – "His will" power. This does not mean that Christians will be immune to temptation. Even Christ was tempted, but the source of His strength was in the Word (Luke 4:1-14), the same source we must use if we are to resist the devil. Like Christ, we are our most vulnerable in our private moments. Whereas He, as our perfect example, resisted, we sometimes commit sins that we think no one sees. However, these private transgressions, if left unchecked, can have far-reaching effects on our relationships in the church, the home and the workplace. Ultimately, these sins will separate us from God.

Now, more than ever, the real serpent in our homes may be the computer with its readily available Internet pornography. A 2000 survey published by *Leadership* magazine found that out of the 89 percent of pastors or preachers who are online, more than one-third of them acknowledged viewing pornography on the Internet ("Pastors").

John Bentley at Freed-Hardeman University conducted a survey of 4,210 Christians about personal viewing habits on the Internet (Bentley).

The results were shocking. Of those participating in the survey, 57 percent of men and 5 percent of women had intentionally viewed pornography. Of those who had intentionally viewed, nearly 1 of 3 men had repeatedly returned to view it again more than 25 times. Seventy-nine percent of men who had viewed pornography online even once said it is now a temptation.

Bentley stated that gender, age, wisdom, hormones, and maturity are all factors, as is demonstrated by the 73 percent of men ages 19 to 29 who said they are tempted to view pornography as compared with only 9 percent of men 60 and over. When we consider that the average age for first seeing a pornographic magazine for males is 11, we must be even more vigilant about unsupervised Internet use by our children. Despite all the filters and other electronic guards we employ – and employ them we must – images will slip through. The best way to guard our children from Internet pornography is through constant personal supervision.

Surely, if temptation could exist in the beginning in Eden, the most perfect paradise on earth, it can exist anywhere in creation today, even in that most perfect institution on earth, the church. That is why we are commanded in Hebrews 10:25 not to forsake "the assembling of ourselves together, as is the manner of some, but [to exhort] one another." The collective influence of a group of Christians is a powerful deterrent to temptation. We must stay close to one another within the Lord's body. Meanwhile, if our private lives have become filled with sin, we need to pray for forgiveness and the strength to resist future temptation. If we can eliminate the source of our temptation or remove ourselves from it, we must immediately do so. However, we must remember, as Christ taught by inference in Matthew 12:43-45, a life swept clean of evil leaves us vulnerable if we do not fill it with the presence of God. We must satiate our private lives with God's Word, or Satan will return to fill our hearts with even more temptations.

Shod With the Preparation of the Gospel

1. List the answers to temptation mentioned in this chapter. Share which method you have found most useful in dealing with one of your personal temptations.

2. How important is prayer to temptation? Read Matthew 6:13 and 26:41.

3. Compare the ideas expressed in Matthew 12:43-45 and 2 Corinthians 4:7-11.

4. Is the free enterprise system of the United States based on the doctrine of humanism? Discuss how our society may or may not promote the philosophy of humanism.

5. Discuss the implications of John Bentley's study of Internet pornography in the church. How can the church combat this insidious sin?

6. What can we learn about the difference in males and females from Bentley's study? How can women help men avoid the temptation of pornography?

7. What are some private temptations that may be pitfalls for females more than for males?

8. In light of Dolly's temptation as a child and her problems with overeating as an adult, was the removal of unhealthy food during her childhood effective training for adulthood? Would another method have been more effective?

Chapter 2

Breached BOUNDARIES

*"O, Lord, I know the way of man is not in himself;
It is not in man who walks to direct his own steps."
(Jeremiah 10:23)*

Barefoot With Dolly

Our house in Ethridge was built beside a paved road that sloped down-hill to the highway. Among the few local automobile owners was my dad. He had a pale green 1946 Dodge, his pride and joy, and in those days it was still exciting to ride with him the six miles to the county seat when he had bank deposits to make. He would turn his general merchandise store over to his clerk and would pick up my mother and me at home to ride with him to Lawrenceburg.

Upon arrival back home, my mother would open her door for me to sit on the broad doorsill, a smaller version of the running board on earlier automobiles, while she and my dad continued to talk. I was not allowed to stray from that rather uncomfortable sitting position on the grooved rubber because we were parked on the edge of the road. The road held danger, and I had been taught never to step off the concrete wall edging our yard onto the gravel shoulder unless I was accompanied by an adult. The wall was my barrier.

No children lived on our side of Ethridge, and because my brother was 9 years older, I was basically an only child left to play alone with my imaginary friends. At the crest of the hill above us and on the other side of the road lived an older couple whose granddaughter visited them on rare occasions. To entice her, I suppose, to visit more frequently, her grandfather built her a playhouse. And what a grand playhouse it was! Its bright white clapboard siding replicated their house in miniature with a green door and a window with green shutters. The roof was a shiny, barn-red tin.

I had no such playhouse. Mine was imaginary. Behind our house along the north wall was a green, mossy rug that I constantly had to sweep clean with my limb broom because of the tiny roofing gravel that fell from the slope above. At one end of the moss was a huge hemlock tree with the limbs removed on the side toward the house so the electric company could read the meter on the wall. Within this hollow area under the tree, a concrete block from my dad's store became my stove, its holes serving as my oven. Mud pies cooked slowly there in the shade to be served up later on my miniature tin dish set. Although I loved to play in this area because it was mossy and cool in the summer, its main attraction was that my mother could not see me from the kitchen window; it was my private haven.

Haven or not, it could in no way compare with the real playhouse in our neighbor's yard. The temptation was more than I could stand. While my mother took her daily afternoon nap, I would creep out to the front yard, descend the steps in the center of the concrete wall, and walk up the middle of the road past the field between our houses to play in that wonderful little house. Of course, as soon as the old couple living there discovered me, they would call my mother to let her know where I was.

My situation was not helped by the fact that my mother was an avid flower gardener. Our yard was filled with irises, peonies, roses and flowering shrubs such as spirea and forsythia, both of which produced excellent switches. Many a time they were picked for just such a purpose. My brother, having heard that salt kills trees, once tried sprinkling these bushes with a shaker from the kitchen table, but to no avail. They only grew more prolifically. We both knew that we could be in for some painful moments when, upon returning home from church, my mother broke off a switch from one of the shrubs lining our driveway as she stepped out of the car.

On the occasions when I took my furtive trek to the top of the hill, my mother would soon arrive with just such a switch in hand and tap me with it on the legs every few steps all the way back to our yard. You would think that one, or maybe two, such trips would have done the trick. But no, I was stubborn and resolute about that playhouse. I thought that if my parents truly loved me, they would build one for me. After all, my dad had all the supplies at his store. So again and again (I do not remember the number of times), I walked up the middle of the road to that playhouse, and again and again, Mother would switch me back home.

Finally, she realized that the switch, however painful, was not doing the trick, so she came up with a new strategy. She took a length of cotton rope and tied it firmly around my waist with the knot in the back then she secured the other end to the clothesline in our backyard. Although I could run up and down the line sideways, I could not leave the premises – which, of course, was mother's intention. This remedy cured me after only one application, especially because it was combined with the impending gloom of night. As the evening wore on and the sky darkened, I begged and pleaded to be let loose to return to the safety of our lighted house. I also promised that I would never again go up the road to the playhouse. And I didn't.

Rest a Spell

1. Did you ever do anything dangerous that got you in trouble as a child? Share your "perils" and the consequences you suffered.
2. What are some dangers that children today face that were not a problem for you as a child?
3. Are there actually more dangers for children, or are we just more paranoid?
4. Is it possible to teach young children about danger (i.e., playing in the road, touching a hot stove) without spanking?
5. What problems do modern parents have with using spanking as discipline that earlier generations did not have? Would a modern parent also have a problem with tethering a child outdoors?
6. What should we fear most for our children?

Walking With the Master

"Something there is that doesn't love a wall," says Robert Frost in his famous poem "Mending Wall" (Frost 47-48). He goes on to reveal a few lines later that he and his neighbor disagree about the necessity of repairing the wall. After all, a wall limits our activities, and most of us don't like to be walled in or walled out. Actually, walls are a visual form of the word "no" – a word that sometimes inspires rebellion and disobedience even when spoken out of love. Therefore, we often take it upon ourselves to breach whatever boundaries are placed in front of us. God's wall is His Word, and staying in His Word will help us fight the wiles of the devil and the perils of the road. Yet our defiant nature makes us step over the line into the world beyond the safety zone.

We are often like the marmot that my husband and I observed on a recent trip up Mt. Evans in Colorado. Marmots are small animals, similar to groundhogs, that live in dens among the rocks and sparse vegetation above the timberline in the Rocky Mountains. This marmot, however, had chosen to build his den in the middle of the paved highway we were traveling. Like a jack-in-the-box, he would suddenly pop up to check for cars, then he would disappear as suddenly if one were coming. Perhaps he had built his den in the winter when the road was closed to traffic only to find out later that he was "living in the fast lane." Similarly, many of us find ourselves living in the fast lane. What a dangerous place to be! We step over the wall of His Word and place our souls in jeopardy. The Bible is full of examples of those who ignored the boundaries established by God to walk a more hazardous path.

• **Lot.** Consider the choice made by Lot in Genesis 13. He was so blinded by the beauty of the Jordan valley with its well-watered pastureland that he failed to show proper deference to Abram who, because of his age and more prominent position as family patriarch, should have been allowed the better choice of land. After all, ownership of Canaan had been promised to Abram, and therefore, it was Abram's land by God-given right. By choosing the valley, Lot also failed to show his gratitude to the kinsman and benefactor who had enriched him on their long and arduous journey. Instead, he greedily chose the best land for himself, blindly ignoring the dangers hidden within that landscape. Then he was not satisfied with the valley itself but drew closer to the action, despite the risks. He "dwelt in the cities of the plain and pitched his tent even as far as Sodom" (Genesis 13:12), thus placing his family in jeopardy.

The results of Lot's choice were disastrous, and he found himself "oppressed by the filthy conduct of the wicked"; they "tormented his righteous soul from day to day [with] their lawless deeds" (2 Peter 2:7-8). Although Lot obviously maintained his own virtue, his choice to live among the ungodly brought calamity to his family and his progeny. Lot offered his two virginal daughters as sexual partners to the perverse Sodomites who desired instead the angels/men who came to warn Lot to leave the city (Genesis 19:6-8). His daughters lost their fiancés who refused to leave Sodom because they thought Lot was only joking about the impending destruction (v. 14), and Lot lost his wife who could not resist the temptation to look back at her home (v. 26). Finally, Lot's daughters committed incest with their father, producing two nations of people, the Moabites and the Ammonites, who later became enemies of God's chosen people (vv. 30-38).

Sometimes we, too, can lose our families through rash decisions. Although it may be impossible to shield our children completely from the sexual perversion in our society today, it is our responsibility as Christian parents to do what we can. Surely the influence of the lifestyles in the city of Sodom had much to do with the later decision of Lot's daughters to commit incest with their father. And just as surely, Lot's willingness to offer them for sex to the Sodomites had its influence on his daughters' loose morals.

Just as the type of food we eat determines our body's health, so do the images and lifestyles surrounding us determine our soul's health. We must be vigilant in our choices of what TV shows, what music, and what movies we allow our children (and ourselves) to view. Homosexuality, premarital sex, masturbation and fellatio are commonly discussed or depicted in today's media. Meanwhile, sexual innuendo abounds through redefined terms that were once used in more innocent ways. Even news shows can indoctrinate us and our children, having taken on a tabloid flavor in an attempt to outsell the competition. How important it is for us to set the right example for our children and, like our heavenly Father, provide a wall of safety within His Word.

• **Jonah.** Another Old Testament character who chose to ignore God and go his own way was Jonah. Like a rebellious child, Jonah actually thought he could run away and hide from God rather than preach in Nineveh (Jonah 1:1-3). God sent him in one direction; Jonah went the opposite. Only after putting a ship and its crew in jeopardy did Jonah finally accept responsibility for his disobedience (v. 12). Lying alone in darkness in the belly of the fish prepared for him by God, he repented and prayed for three days and nights (2:1-9). Repentance is defined for us in the example of Jonah. Not only did he ask forgiveness, but he also immediately turned around and went to Nineveh to preach as God had commanded him earlier (3:3).

Like Jonah, we too must suffer dark and lonely days before we realize that we are out of bounds, running away from God. His discipline turns us around and brings us to repentance. Hebrews 12 explains clearly that although discipline is never pleasant at the time, God's discipline is necessary if we are to grow into the Christians He wants us to be (v. 11). It is always out of His love for us as His children (v. 6) that He chastises us. In fact, if God chose not to correct us, it would be a sign that we are illegitimate children of the world, not members of His family for whom He cares (v. 8).

When dark days come as a result of our failure as Christians, and we all do fail at times, we must seek God and ask forgiveness as Jonah did. God's loving arms are always longer than any distance we place between ourselves and Him. Because God is our Father who loves us, His forgiveness will be freely given to us if we ask, and the result in our lives will be for our ultimate good.

Jesus said, "What man is there among you who, if his son asks for bread, will give him a stone? Or if he asks for a fish, will he give him a serpent? If you then, being evil, know how to give good gifts to your children, how much more will your Father who is in heaven give good things to those who ask Him!" (Matthew 7:9-11). Humble, contrite prayer for forgiveness closes the gap in the wall that we have breached, and we are at home with God once more.

Because God's love is the archetype for our father-child relationships on earth, we as parents must follow His pattern in loving and disciplining our children. The wall we place around them is reassuring because it says we care enough to say, "No." Many children today, even those with Christian parents, have few clearly established boundaries, and without them the children are confused. If we leave them exposed, the depravity of the world will conflict with what our children hear from their Bible school teachers and the pulpit. Sadly, a father who fails to be the spiritual leader in his home and protect his children from the world when they are young may later come to regret the years of training his children missed. How tragic for that father to see his children leave the Lord because of his immaturity and failure as a Christian parent.

The wayward son in Christ's parable left the safety of his father's house to travel in the broad "way that leads to destruction" (Matthew 7:13) where he "wasted his possessions with prodigal living" (Luke 15:13). It is not surprising that the broad, fast lane has not changed much over the centuries.

Today the emphasis is still on having fun and being in the popular crowd at all costs. The mother who is more interested in her daughter or son's being popular and fitting in with the more affluent crowd at school rather than with the youth group at church may later regret pushing her child in the wrong direction when, as an adult, he or she values social status more than the Lord. Obsession with designer clothes, sports cars and the latest technological fad can lead only to grief. I shall never forget defending a Christian teenager to her high school teacher by pointing out that the girl was running with the wrong crowd. Imagine my chagrin when, with a skeptical lift of her eyebrow, the teacher replied, "Have you ever considered that she *is* the wrong crowd?"

If our children are prayerfully loved and disciplined according to God's Word, they will not stray so far that they never return to Him and us (Proverbs 22:6). The wayward son in Christ's parable found his way home. When his money ran out, he realized that, unlike his father, the world cared nothing for him. At his lowest, darkest hour working in a pig sty, he remembered the love, protection and safety within the walls of his home. In humility, he repented and turned his footsteps toward home, asking and receiving his father's forgiveness (Luke 15:14-32).

The Preacher in Ecclesiastes says, "I have seen all the works that are done under the sun; and indeed, all is vanity and grasping for the wind" (1:14). Lest we choose the broad way, perhaps never to return to the safety offered in the arms of Jesus, let us heed the words of Jeremiah: "O, Lord, I know the way of man is not in himself; it is not in man who walks to direct his own steps" (10:23). Just as God held Israel close to Him with "cords of human kindness, with ties of love" (Hosea 11:4 NIV), we too need to stay tethered to Christ, safe within the borders of His kingdom, through our prayer, our worship and our study of His Word.

Shod With the Preparation of the Gospel

1. We sometimes have problems understanding how God disciplines us. Discuss Hebrews 12:5-11 and James 1:13-15 as they relate to our being disciplined by God.
2. How do Lot's offering his daughters to the Sodomites and his daughters' choice of incest demonstrate a lack of faith in God's providence?
3. What are some situations Christians face today that require faith in God's providence to escape?
4. The father in Jesus' parable (Luke 15:11-32) allowed his son to make a wrong choice. When should we allow our children to make bad choices?
5. Discuss how Samson breached the boundaries God set for him. What wrong choices did he make (Judges 13–16)?
6. How separate from the world should we be? How separate was Christ? See 1 John 2:15-17.

Chapter 3

Covetousness

VS. **CONTENTMENT**

"Now godliness with contentment is great gain. For we brought nothing into this world, and it is certain we can carry nothing out. And having food and clothing, with these we shall be content."
(1 Timothy 6:6-8)

Barefoot With Dolly

As a child I had a gluttonous desire for presents. It might have been because I felt so deprived. My parents had stringent rules about gift giving, especially when it came to toys. As they saw it, such frivolous gifts were appropriate only one time of year, and that was Christmas. What was worse, they obviously told Santa Claus the number of toys he could leave me: I was allowed only a doll and one other toy. Gifts of clothing from my family made up the rest of my loot and included an annual pair of socks from my aunt, who worked in a sock factory. How unfair it all seemed; how meager the reward for a year's worth of good behavior.

The one gift accompanying the doll was always age appropriate. Before I reached school age, I received wooden blocks with letters painted on them and a tin dish set with miniature cups and saucers imprinted with Little Bo Peep. Not as exciting was the blue iron that foretold my job later as official handkerchief ironer for my dad. About the time I started to school, a metal dollhouse appeared, its rooms already furnished with painted rugs and wall decor and movable plastic furniture in pink, blue and yellow. By the time I was 10, I was old enough to receive a baseball pinball game, complete with a spring-loaded plunger, metal ball bearings to shoot, and battery operated lights – all housed under a breakable glass top. And, finally, at age 12, I received my first record player. I can name all these gifts over the years because there were so few of them.

In the primary grades, I would return to school in January bringing my doll. The other children, who I thought were more privileged, would bring several toys to school and brag about the pile at home that Santa had left them. Obviously, I wasn't on his "good kid" list. I was very upset with Santa Claus and with my parents, who obviously hadn't mailed him my letters (I had even drawn the stamp on).

When I was 10 years old, I thought I had hit the jackpot. I opened the door to the living room on Christmas morning to find a whole room full of dolls staring back at me. They were seated on the sofa, on the matching armchair, on the occasional chair, and on the piano bench. Each one was different. One had curly blonde hair and a Shirley Temple smile above the white lace collar of her blue cotton dress. One had painted blue eyes, painted brown hair and painted fat pink cheeks on her breakable chalk head attached to the neck of her stuffed muslin body. Another doll's moveable eyes drooped as if embarrassed by her simple yellow print dress made from a feed sack. Largest of all was a full-size baby doll made of soft rubber and dressed in a white flannel gown, her lips pursed and waiting for a bottle. A variety of other dolls completed the scene. I was ecstatic; for a moment my insatiable desire for gifts was replete.

Then I realized that something was wrong with this picture. I was being duped! These were not new dolls at all. The curly blonde in the blue dress was last year's doll. The painted chalk doll had a chip in her brown hair and was missing a finger. Yes, her dress was new, but I had played with her when I was 4 years old. The embarrassed doll, whose drooping eyes were incapacitated by age and use, was even older than the painted one; and the baby doll's legs were bruised with permanent grass stains from years of outdoor play. What had Santa done to me? My mother was culpable as well, for I could recognize her handiwork with the sewing machine; some of my dresses were made from the same fabrics.

It is true that I should have been thankful that my mother had taken so much time to redress all my old dolls, but I wasn't. Instead, my greedy eyes were searching for a new doll among the old. I found her, in the middle of the sofa, her white satin bride's dress gleaming clean and pure, her bright blue eyes smiling at me through the veil attached to the flowers in her hair, and in her right hand a bouquet with streaming ribbons. Little did I know that she was the beginning of a series of dolls with which I could not actually play. She and her sisters, who came the next two years in their pink and blue tulle-over-satin dresses, were to be enjoyed as they sat primly on the bedspread against the pillow on my bed.

About this same time my mother decided I was getting too old to give Santa all the credit. I clung to the myth with all my being – as I also did the tooth fairy, elves under toadstools, and whatever was under my bed after dark that would grab me if I let my hand hang over the side. Mother hinted about Santa, saying that he was getting a new set of false teeth. Now I knew that my dad was going through a painful time at the dentist having all his teeth pulled, but I refused to put the two together in my mind. However, reality set in when I crawled under my parents' bed to find my next new doll and a pair of house slippers in a shoe box just days before Christmas. I gave up. It truly hadn't been Santa's fault that I had received so few presents each Christmas. Just as I should have known it was all my parents' doing.

Rest a Spell

1. What were your Christmases like when you were growing up? Did you believe in Santa Claus?
2. How did your family deal with the myth of Santa Claus? Can believing in Santa Claus have a detrimental effect on a child's faith in God in adulthood?
3. What one gift did you receive that stands out as a favorite memory?
4. Are too many gifts harmful to a child's spiritual growth? How many are too many?
5. How do we curb greed for an abundance of things in our children?
6. What was the best gift Dolly received for Christmas in this story?

Walking With the Master

Dr. William Jeter, my dentist, had six precocious children. They were a very active bunch. Once on vacation, he even lost one at a filling station and had to drive back to get her. All of them were varied in their interests and abilities, which resulted in a variety of occupations in adulthood: two nurses, an occupational therapist, a lawyer, an airline pilot, and a Tony award-winning actor. However, they had one thing in common – a desire for "stuff." When they were growing up, Dr. Jeter would periodically threaten to make an appointment with a surgeon to get their "wants" cut out.

Maybe we all should have our "wants" cut out. The materialistic society of today says, "I want it all – now!" The opulent world of the rich and famous is spread like a gourmet feast for all the world to see via the media – designer dresses, diamond necklaces, sports cars, yachts, mansions – and Americans of lesser means try to follow suit. Our culture has become so commercialized that all of us feel we must have the latest electronic gadgets, the trendiest clothing styles, the most stylish automobiles, and a house with enough superfluous square footage to start a motel business. Families spend exorbitant amounts to put on a show of pseudo-wealth while racking up, as a nation, $915.5 billion ($3,020 per every man, woman and child in the United States) in credit card debt (Amadeo).

Our possessions now possess us. Consider an item that most of us find a necessity today: the cell phone. Although it is a wonderful tool for keeping up with our children's whereabouts, we now let inconsequential calls interrupt our business meetings, our meals, our leisure-time activities, our personal face-to-face conversations and even our worship. Our bosses have gotten in on the action, handing out cell phones, pagers and BlackBerrys so that employees are on-call 24 hours a day rather than from 9 to 5. We may have liberated our phones from a cord, but we have ensnared ourselves and lost our freedom.

Meanwhile, we do not realize how all the little luxuries of life eat away at our budgets. Do you drink bottled water on a daily basis? Five bottles a week add up to $390 per year. Do you like those lattes and special coffees? Drink them five times a week and take $650+ from your annual income. Technology, too, takes a sizeable nip: the average cost of a cable subscription, TiVo service, high-speed Internet, and cell phone equals $2,000+ a year. Many add another $1,000 or so for satellite radio, premium cable channels, Netflix and downloaded music on an iPod (Steinriede E1). These services, even when bundled, can overwhelm a struggling family who may not realize how much they cut into the family budget. We can survive without most or all of these costly luxuries – and they are luxuries – by "unbundling" ourselves from the burden they place on us.

Little luxuries are often just another way to perpetuate the facade of elitism. How we are perceived by our peers has become more important than who – and Whose – we really are. Much of our lives today is dedicated to impressing others. Perhaps in no other way is this more evident than in the modern wedding. Although large weddings have always been in vogue, today's weddings are over the top. A wedding planner has taken the place of a family member or friend, and websites are now dedicated to promoting the couple's big day. Only a decade or two ago, a wedding reception consisted of cake, mints, nuts and a drink. Now guests come expecting a full sit-down meal with entertainment. The latest twist is a hired choreographer to plan a song-and-dance routine performed for the "audience" by the bride and groom and their attendants. All these extras have now piled up to a whopping $27,000 average cost for weddings in the United States.

Essayist Mary Beth Baptiste, who rebelled by getting married for $150, points out that if the average cost is multiplied by the 2.3 million weddings annually, $64 billion a year is spent by Americans on weddings – more than the gross domestic product of many small countries including Iceland, Lithuania, Nepal and Luxembourg (14). These elaborate productions staged for everyone's enjoyment put undue stress on the bride and groom and often take a toll on the ensuing marriage.

Is it wrong to have a large wedding, to own a nice house, or to indulge in luxuries? No, not as long as we can truly afford them while keeping our priorities straight – Jesus first, others second, and ourselves last. God has never condemned the rich for being rich; rather, He has condemned the wicked motives and skewed priorities that often accompany riches. First Timothy 6:10 does not say that "money is a root of all kinds of evil"; rather it is "the love of money" and the things it can buy that are the true sin. The Old Testament tells us of many commendable men of God who managed to be rich and faithful at the same time. Abraham was a very rich man in "livestock, in silver, and in gold" (Genesis 13:2), and Job possessed so much that he was considered "the greatest of all the people of the East" (Job 1:3). Later, in the New Testament, a rich and sinful tax collector, Zacchaeus, wanted to see Jesus so badly that he compensated for his short stature by climbing a tree, thus repenting and changing his usurious practices (Luke 19:2-9). Joseph, a rich man of Arimathea who had become a follower of Jesus, asked Pilate for His body and buried it in his own tomb (Matthew 27:57-60). Although none of these rich men was perfect, they had their priorities in order by putting their faith in God before their possessions.

It is still possible to be rich and at the same time put God first. In the last century, A.M. Burton gave away nearly all of the millions he earned to the Lord's work (Pullias), and there are Christians today who recognize their riches as a blessing from God and place Him first by putting their resources to use in a similar fashion. Sadly, these examples are few. The Bible warns that the rich are more vulnerable to temptation than the poor. Jesus said that "it is easier for a camel to go through the eye of a needle than for a rich man to enter the kingdom of God" (Matthew 19:24).

We Americans of lesser means, who are nevertheless rich in the world's eyes, must not think that God's warnings do not apply to us. Through our desire to have the same abundance of material things that the ultra-rich can afford, we may be even more guilty of "the love of money" than those who are richer than we. This desire for abundance often leads to a life spent laboring for the wrong reasons and the wrong goals. Proverbs 23:4-5 warns against wasting our time pursuing riches: "Do not overwork to be rich; Because of your own understanding, cease! Will you set your eyes on that which is not? For riches certainly make themselves wings; They fly away like an eagle toward heaven." Such a pursuit has no end, because the more we have, the more we want. John D. Rockefeller was once asked, "How much money does someone need to be fully satisfied?" His answer was "a little more than what he has" ("Money" 392). It is also true that the more we have, the more it takes to live. The Preacher tells us, "When goods increase, They increase who eat them; So what profit have the owners Except to see them with their eyes?" He even adds a further price paid by the rich: sleep deprivation (Ecclesiastes 5:11-12). Similarly, Haggai points to the futility of gaining wealth: "Consider your ways! You have sown much, and bring in little; You eat, but do not have enough; You drink, but you are not filled with drink; You clothe yourselves, but no one is warm; And he who earns wages, Earns wages to put into a bag with holes" (1:5-6).

Therefore, we must all heed the words of warning throughout the Scriptures about placing our emphasis in life on material gain. Psalm 10 warns us that our prosperity can lead us away from God: "The wicked in his proud countenance does not seek God; God is in none of his thoughts … He has said in his heart, 'God has forgotten; He hides His face; He will never see' " (vv. 4, 11). Similarly, Jesus warned in the parable of the sower that the cares of the world and "the deceitfulness of riches choke the word" when it has been planted in our hearts, resulting in unfruitfulness (Matthew 13:22). Jesus also instructs us not to gather up treasures on earth but to lay up for ourselves treasures in heaven. "For where your treasure is, there your heart will be also" (6:19-21).

One of the saddest stories in the Gospels is that of the rich young ruler who could not part with his possessions to follow Christ (Matthew 19:16-22). Sad, too, is the absence of contentment and happiness in our lives because we have lost sight of the essence of life. As Paul Lee Tan puts it, "Money can buy a bed but not sleep. Books but not brains. Food but not an appetite. Finery but not beauty. A house but not a home. Medicine but not health. Pleasures but not peace. Luxuries but not culture. Amusements but not joy. A crucifix but not a Savior. A church building but not heaven" ("Money" 391). True happiness can never come from the things we own. True happiness can come only from serving the Lord. This is the conclusion that the Preacher ultimately comes to in Ecclesiastes 12:13: "Fear God and keep His commandments, For this is man's all." Hopefully, we can grow to the point in our spirituality that we can say with David, "The law of Your mouth is better to me Than thousands of coins of gold and silver" (Psalm 119:72).

The only difference in the glass in a window through which we can see the needs of others and the glass in a mirror in which we see only ourselves is the silver. God's law requires that we turn away from our self-absorption and open the windows of our hearts to those in need. We must see not only their plight but act as well. "But whoever has this world's goods, and sees his brother in need, and shuts up his heart from him, how does the love of God abide in him?" (1 John 3:17).

In the early days of the church, Barnabas, the "son of encouragement," demonstrated his love for God by selling his land to help others (Acts 4:36-37), and Paul commanded the Corinthian church to "lay something aside" on the first day of the week for the relief of the Jerusalem saints (1 Corinthians 16:2). In both cases, money was given collectively to the church to help others, but as individuals we can also perform charitable deeds as needs arise. However, we must be careful that the glory goes to God and not to us personally. Although not always possible, if we give in secret, God will reward us openly (Matthew 6:1-4). In fact, we can never out-give God. Christ said, "Give, and it will be given to you: good measure, pressed down, shaken together, and running over will be put into your bosom. For with the same measure that you use, it will be measured back to you" (Luke 6:38). Although God may choose to reward us with earthly treasures, He knows the kind of wealth we need. It may be a reward of good health, a peaceable family life, or Christian friends. Ultimately, his gifts will lead to contentment.

True contentment comes to us only when we totally commit our lives and possessions to God, trusting Him to take care of us. Paul told Timothy, "Now godliness with contentment is great gain. For we brought nothing into this world, and it is certain we can carry nothing out. And having food and clothing, with these we shall be content" (1 Timothy 6:6-8). Paul himself found such contentment: "I have learned in whatever state I am, to be content: I know how to be abased, and I know how to abound. Everywhere and in all things I have learned both to be full and to be hungry, both to abound and to suffer need. I can do all things through Christ who strengthens me" (Philippians 4:11-13).

We should strive for balance in our lives and possessions – not too much, not too little. Proverbs 30:7-9 is the perfect prayer for the Christian life: "Two things I request of You (Deprive me not before I die): Remove falsehood and lies far from me; Give me neither poverty nor riches – Feed me with the food allotted to me; Lest I be full and deny You, and say, 'Who is the Lord?' Or lest I be poor and steal, and profane the name of my God."

A very prosperous man stooped to pick up a penny from the sidewalk. His employees who were accompanying him were surprised. None of them had deigned to pick up such a meager amount of change. The rich man explained his actions: "I always pick up a lost penny. On it are written some very important words, 'In God we trust.' By looking at the penny, I am reminded that I am lost without God, and it is in Him I trust – not money." Trusting in God as the source of all our blessings will lead to contentment and happiness. Our "wants" will be excised to be replaced by a giving heart.

Shod With the Preparation of the Gospel

1. How much are you affected by the latest trends in fashion (i.e., clothes, accessories, cosmetics)?
2. Sit in your favorite room in your home. Make a list of all the necessities in the room. Then make a list of the nonessential items. What do the decor and nonessential items say about you and your preferences? Are all nonessential items luxuries? Why or why not?
3. Do you have a collection of any kind? If so, what do you collect? Why do you collect these items?
4. What little luxury do you indulge in on a regular basis? What little luxury could you give up to divert the money to the Lord's work?
5. Examine the scriptures that follow. Summarize each one and decide if the principle it teaches is applicable to society today. Discuss.
   • James 5:1-5
   • Isaiah 2:7-8
   • Ecclesiastes 2:1-12
   • Psalm 37:7-10
   • Luke 16:13
   • 2 Timothy 3:1-5

Chapter 4

Gifting vs. GIVING

"Prepare your generous gift beforehand ... that it may be ready as a matter of generosity and not as a grudging obligation." (2 Corinthians 9:5)

Barefoot With Dolly

I had the misfortune of being born in January – too close to Christmas to receive gifts for my birthday. In my parents' eyes, I had already been indulged enough with my two Santa Claus gifts and new clothes. I simply would have had no celebration at all had it not been for sharing close birthdays with two other children in my class. Faye was born on Jan. 25, J.W. on the 26th, and I on the 27th. This made it convenient for the teacher because one birthday party could suffice for three.

In the lower grades, some parents brought cupcakes for the whole class on their children's birthdays. I have no doubt that my mother wouldn't have carried out this tradition had it not been for Faye and J.W., who rode a bus to school from some distance. Not wanting to disappoint them, she arrived in the second-grade room with frosted cupcakes on J.W.'s birthday, the middle day of the three-day celebration.

Needless to say, my mother was very popular with all the kids in my class. She practiced equal opportunity before it became politically correct. Not only was it important to share a birthday, but it was also important not to be uppity. We could have afforded store-bought clothes, but why buy what you can make for yourself? Besides, ready-made dresses were a rarity in my class. On Valentine's Day, all my classmates got a valentine personally addressed and signed by me, no matter whether they were rich or poor, naughty or nice, from the wrong or the right side of the tracks. To have left someone out was simply unacceptable.

Being almost an only child, I found it galling to share my birthday at school and have no family celebration of the event. At home, it was just another day. In light of my mother's usual inattention to the occasion and the fact that I knew not to cross certain lines that she strictly enforced with a switch, it is no small wonder that I so brazenly crossed that line in the third grade. Because no cupcakes arrived on Friday and my birthday fell on Sunday, I told the teacher that I had a special message for the class from my mother. Rising from my seat, I boldly announced, "You are all invited to our house tomorrow afternoon for my birthday party." Of course, my mother had said no such thing.

I don't recall, but I probably fidgeted all night composing the words to let my mother know that some or all of 27 kids would arrive the next afternoon at our house for a party about which she knew nothing. I am also quite sure that I delayed as long as possible on Saturday morning before finding the courage to relay this important piece of information to her. And had it not been for all those children coming, I am sure that she would have chastised me severely with both tongue and switch for announcing the event without her knowledge. Perhaps she felt guilty for having never given me a party. Whatever her reasons, she hit the kitchen in a whirl of activity and produced a cake in record time along with a large pitcher of lemonade.

When the children arrived at the door, I invited them in. We went to the backyard for games that my mother directed with little or no preparation and some very fast thinking. There were even prizes for the winners. The parents of the students who attended had to do some fast preparation too, I am sure. Most of my presents were items that more than likely were kept on hand: bottles of glue with rubber tips, pencils, boxes of crayons, and a coloring book or two. Actually, it turned out to be a great birthday party, especially because it was my only birthday party.

Although the gifts were small, they were gifts to play with – much better than the one item I received every birthday from my dad. He would bring a rectangular sheet of paper home each year with my name written on it in ink and a number like $50 or $100 or $500, all depending on the prosperity of his business from the previous year. I couldn't even keep that piece of paper. It was taken the next day to the bank where it was placed in a safe drawer. No fun there!

Only when I married at age 22 did I come to appreciate those little pieces of paper as each of the U.S. savings bonds matured. They provided my husband and me with a fine nest egg to begin our life together.

Rest a Spell

1. How important were birthdays in your home while growing up? How important are they to you today?
2. Children born close to Christmas often think their birthdays get overshadowed by this major holiday. How can their parents remedy the situation?
3. Dolly later discovered a news article from the local paper about an elaborate birthday party for her older brother when he turned 3. Do older siblings get more attention than younger ones?
4. Although Dolly's mother may seem overly strict by today's standards, what are some of her parenting traits in this story and in Chapter 3, "The Christmas Surprise," that we can admire and emulate?
5. Do you agree that the gift given by Dolly's father was better than giving her another toy?

Walking With the Master

The story is told about two brothers who re-gifted a pair of pants at Christmas for several years. One brother wrapped the pants around a car tire and drove through snow and ice before placing them in a fancy, beribboned box to give to his brother. He got the pants back the next year with a sledge hammer. His brother had placed the pants in wet concrete to "set." The first brother returned the pants the next Christmas inside a framed wall of a shed; the shed had to be demolished to get to the pants ("Gifts" 229). Why did they resort to such bizarre giving? Perhaps it was for the same reason that my father-in-law gave his presents in unique Christmas tree ornaments. The gifts were always the same: a crisp, new $20 bill for his children and a $10 bill for his grandchildren. It wasn't the gift that counted – it was the packaging of that gift. One year it was empty walnut shells painted gold and glued back together with the money inside; another year it was scrap lumber, the money clamped tightly between two boards fastened together with screws. We had to work for our money. Like the brothers, my father-in-law was attempting to put the fun back into obligatory giving at Christmas.

• **Gifting.** Many of our gifts should be classified as gifting, not giving. The difference in gifting and giving is dependent upon the purpose of the gift, our attitude toward giving, and, more importantly, how much of ourselves we invest in the gift. Giving is so commercialized and impersonal today that we more often than not give only because it is expected. Thus, giving is degraded to gifting.

Perhaps gifting is at its worst before a wedding. We often receive an invitation to a wedding shower for someone we hardly know. Add to that the selections pre-chosen by the bride – either listed online or spit out by a machine at a department store where the gift is then wrapped and sent directly to the shower with a card we did not write – and we have the ultimate in mechanized gifting. How sad it is that we have let convenience replace the joy that comes from investing ourselves in a gift offered with a loving heart.

Obligatory presents are nothing new, but our purpose and attitude determine whether we are truly giving or merely gifting. Monarchs or rulers have always been feted with gifts. Kings in Old Testament days received gifts of tribute, especially if they inspired fear. Uzziah [Azariah], who became king of Judah at age 16 and reigned for 52 years, became so powerful that the neighboring Ammonites brought him gifts (2 Chronicles 26:8). Likewise, Hezekiah, after the defeat of Sennacherib, was honored with gifts because God was obviously on his side (32:20-23).

The most elaborate gifts, however, occurred years earlier during the reign of Solomon when the queen of Sheba brought tribute, perhaps in honor of a trade agreement. She arrived in Jerusalem "with a very great retinue" (1 Kings 10:2), and the ships of Hiram brought so much special wood that the Bible says, "There never again came such almug wood, nor has the like been seen to this day" (10:12). Even in this modern age when a foreign dignitary visits the White House, extravagant gifts are presented to the president. Because of our democratic form of government, he is not allowed to keep the gifts for his personal use and ownership; instead they become the property of the U.S. government. Similarly, if we stay in someone's home, it is customary for us to present our host with a gift. Actually, we are exchanging a tangible gift for the generous giving of hospitality. Again our attitude toward our host and the personal gratitude we feel determines whether we are gifting or giving. Surely our host's generosity in opening her home is giving at its best because of the time and effort she has devoted to our comfort and entertainment. Hospitality is greatly praised in God's Word. Consider the Shunammite woman who not only opened her home to Elisha but went the extra mile by furnishing a room just for his use whenever he was traveling in the vicinity (2 Kings 4:8-10). Elisha repaid her most generously by restoring life to her son through God's power (vv. 32-37). His was truly a gift from the heart.

Sometimes gifts accompany an apology or an entreaty for forgiveness. A gift, we hope, adds the sauce of sincerity to the crow we must eat for some regretful deed or, more frequently, for words we have flippantly spoken without forethought. Gifts mend fences; however, they must be accompanied by apologetic words spoken from a sincere, contrite heart.

Jacob, upon returning to his homeland, was anxious about the reception he would receive from his brother, Esau, especially because he had threatened to kill Jacob 20 years earlier for stealing their father's blessing (Genesis 27:41). Jacob presented gifts before asking the pardon of his estranged brother, "For he said, 'I will appease him with the present that goes before me, and afterward I will see his face; perhaps he will accept me' " (32:20). Esau's reaction to his brother's return was more gracious than Jacob could have hoped. Jacob bowed seven times before Esau who "embraced him, and fell on his neck and kissed him, and they wept" (33:4). When Esau refused his gifts, Jacob insisted that he keep them, saying, "I have seen your face as though I had seen the face of God, and you were pleased with me. Please, take my blessing that is brought to you" (vv. 10-11). The sincerity with which the gift was given was evident and reunited the two brothers.

Sometimes gifts and an apology spoken by a third party can avert disaster. Such was the case of Abigail, the wife of Nabal, who prevented the slaughter of her entire household by David and his 400 warriors in retaliation for the insults spoken by her abusive, ill-mannered husband

(1 Samuel 25). Although she could not change the evil nature of her husband, she did what she could, acting as an ambassador for peace. She brought gifts and words of praise to David, begging him not to attack her home. David replied, "Go up in peace to your house. See, I have heeded your voice and respected your person" (v. 35). Abigail returned home, but Nabal was too drunk to hear what she had accomplished. When he sobered up the next morning, her unappreciative husband flew into such a rage that "his heart died within him, and he became like a stone" – in other words, he had a stroke or heart attack from which he died 10 days later (vv. 37-38). The Lord blessed Abigail and David, who were married soon after these events.

Proverbs 18:16 says, "A gift opens the way for the giver and ushers him into the presence of the great" (NIV). The gifts that Jacob and Abigail gave truly opened "the way" for them in the same way that a thoughtfully chosen gift, accompanied by a genuine apology, will unlock closed doors for us today.

In contrast, the writer of Proverbs condemns bribery (6:35) as does the old law (Deuteronomy 16:18-19). Bribery is a gift offered as a cover for a hidden agenda. It is born in disguise and conceived by greed, a guilty conscience, and/or fear of retribution. It may be an offer to wash dishes by a teenager before her father receives a letter announcing her suspension from school. It may be new artwork on a grandmother's refrigerator before she discovers that all the "not-before-dinner" cookies have disappeared from the jar. Bribery, however, dons a more serious mask when it is gifted by adults. It may be jewelry from a husband who is attracted to a pretty co-worker, home-cooked meals from a wife who has maxed out all her credit cards, new iPods at Christmas from the boss who knows that pink slips will go out in January, or even an idle promise of better health benefits from a politician who wants his constituents' votes. Many times, these gifts come wrapped in flattery pretending to be a compliment. Bribery and deceit are gifting at its worst.

• **Giving.** So, what is giving? It is a gift in which we have invested time, effort and thought and presented cheerfully and generously with a genuine purpose in mind. Ultimately, it is a gift born of love. God is the ultimate giver. He gives us temporal gifts: food, clothing and shelter. In His most famous sermon, Jesus tells us not to worry about these necessities because they will be supplied to meet our needs (Matthew 6:25-34). We are also promised that "while the earth remains, Seedtime and harvest, Cold and heat, Winter and summer, And day and night shall not cease" (Genesis 8:22). More importantly, God gives us spiritual gifts. He is the giver of true wisdom (James 1:5; 3:17), He is the giver of grace (James 4:6), He is the giver of salvation (Ephesians 2:8-9), and He is the giver of eternal life (Romans 6:23). The list could go on and on. His greatest gift, of course, was given out of love for us: "For God so loved the world that He gave His only begotten Son, that whoever believes in Him should not perish but have everlasting life" (John 3:16). Jesus Christ is the greatest gift of all, for through Him we have salvation.

If God loved us enough to sacrifice His Son and if Jesus willingly gave His life for the forgiveness of our sins, then we, as receivers of this gift, must manifest our love for others through our generosity. We are particularly admonished to take care of the poor. Proverbs 22:9 says, "He who has a generous eye will be blessed, For he gives of his bread to the poor." We sometimes excuse ourselves from this mission of mercy by blaming the poor for being poor. "If they would just get a job and work," we say, or, "They are lazy and just want a handout." We drop our Christian duty onto the shoulders of the government as we practice the philosophy of the priest and Levite in the parable of the good Samaritan: out of sight, out of mind (Luke 10:25-37). According to the Word, as children of God we cannot look the other way and ignore the poor. "He who gives to the poor will not lack, But he who hides his eyes will have many curses" (Proverbs 28:27). Furthermore, our giving must come from a heart of love; otherwise, it is of no profit (1 Corinthians 13:3).

Giving is commanded as an act of worship to God. However, God does not want our thoughtless gifting of the spare change left over from what He has already given us. The widow who gave her two coins, all she had, was praised by Jesus in contrast to the wealthy worshipers who gifted a small portion of their goods (Luke 21:1-4). Giving, remember, not only requires purpose (forethought) and the right attitude (cheerfulness) but also an investment of self (liberality). Paul commends the Corinthian church who "had previously promised" what they would give and instructs them to have the gift ready "as a matter of generosity and not as a grudging obligation." Their giving served two purposes: it supplied the needs of fellow Christians, and it served as a way to say thanks to God for His generous gifts (2 Corinthians 9:5-15), especially for "His indescribable gift" (v. 15). Paul establishes the type of giving God wants: "So let each one give as he purposes in his heart, not grudgingly or of necessity; for God loves a cheerful giver" (v. 7).

Although reward should not be our incentive, giving, rather than gifting, will yield rich returns. This promise was made centuries ago through the prophet Isaiah:

> If you extend your soul to the hungry
> And satisfy the afflicted soul,
> Then your light shall dawn in the darkness,
> And your darkness shall be as the noonday.
> The Lord will guide you continually,
> And satisfy your soul in drought,
> And strengthen your bones;
> You shall be like a watered garden,
> And like a spring of water, whose waters do not fail. (58:10-11)

Shod With the Preparation of the Gospel

1. What are some situations today that lead to gifting rather than giving? Do you find yourself gifting more than giving? How can we personalize our obligatory gifting so that it becomes giving?
2. Have you ever given a gift as an apology for the actions of someone else? Was it effective?
3. Why is hospitality important to the Lord's church today? Have we reduced the effectiveness of hospitality by hosting events at church rather than at home? How often do you have others in your home?
4. Jesus said, "The poor you will always have with you" (Matthew 26:11 NIV). Discuss these verses: Proverbs 10:4; 14:20; 20:13; 21:17; and 2 Thessalonians 3:10. Contrast them with Proverbs 14:31; 21:13; 31:20; and James 2:1-9.
5. Discuss the two givers contrasted in Romans 5:15-18. What is the "free gift"?
6. In today's materialistic climate, how can we teach our children that it is better to give than to receive?

Chapter 5

"Let each of you look out not only for his own interests, but also for the interests of others."
(Philippians 2:4)

Barefoot With Dolly

It probably wasn't fair to my 9-year-old brother, Corky, to be suddenly presented with a baby sister. Although I was later told how excited he was over my birth, I know I grew up to be a pest he barely tolerated at times.

It's a wonder I survived birth and my first year. My parents were stuck in a ditch on a country road the day before I was born, and "birthin' babies" was not one of my dad's talents. I waited, however, until after midnight and came into this world in the local sanitarium (I'm not kidding!), where so many babies had been born that all the beds were taken, and I was placed in a cardboard box. My dad, being proud of his baby daughter, went out immediately and bought the hospital a new bed to put me in. My mother, at 36, had a difficult time after my birth, so my dad took over my care for several weeks. Fortunately, my aunt stopped him from accidentally feeding me the starch (intended for the clothes) instead of the formula I was supposed to drink.

Although my brother may have enjoyed the novelty of a baby sister for a while, my presence began to pall as I grew older. We were quite different in temperament, made more so by our age difference. Our years together were short; he left for college when I was 9. He was stuck often as my baby sitter when our parents were occupied for short periods elsewhere. I totally trusted him in my younger years, a mistake that got me hurt a few times. He taught me as a 5-year-old to catch honeybees by their wings when they lit on the butterfly bush in our backyard. He hoped to paint their tails as an experiment to see if they would return to the same source for honey. Naively, I followed his instructions. Another time I stood on the opposite end of our long back porch while he knocked down a wasp nest on the other side; he wasn't stung, but I was.

We fought over everything. On cold Sunday mornings, we would rush to hunker down in front of the Thermador electric heater to warm our backs. It was a constant push and shove to get the most heat until we were commanded to get quiet. When our parents were not there and my brother was left alone to boss me around, we really had our tussles. Of course, I was an expert tattletale without seeming to be so. In his senior year of high school, he hit me in the head with his fist, leaving a small bruise from his new class ring. Wanting to gain my mother's sympathy and clearly set blame on my brother, I painted the scar on my forehead with the most obvious medicine I knew – tincture of Merthiolate from the medicine cabinet. I met Mother before she could even get in the door, and, of course, the shiny red splotch on my forehead elicited the expected inquiry: "What happened?" Before I could finish my explanation, my brother, not to be outdone, returned from the bathroom with a red bull's-eye painted on his arm around the tiny place where I had scratched him in retaliation.

Sometimes, however, we were on the same team, he being the leader with me as his trusty sidekick. My brother pre-dated the electronic age and was quite a genius when it came to all things mechanical. Our parents had bought him a wire recorder (not realizing that technology would favor tape, and wire would become obsolete) which led him to an idea ahead of its time. Corky hooked up the wire recorder to an alarm clock and the radio so that it would automatically record a radio show. On one occasion while our parents were gone from home, he strung wires in the attic to make the radio signal better. As he stood on top of the stepladder with his head through the attic entry, he knocked over a lamp that he had borrowed from beside our parents' bed. Picking up the broken pieces of the globe, he placed them strategically on the floor around the nightstand. Our lie was to be that he had been looking for a magazine and had accidentally broken the lamp. Trying to be helpful, I also sprinkled some powder from our mother's talcum box to make the scene look even more authentic. I was prepared to stand behind my brother's story.

Imagine my dismay when he told Mother the truth before he went to bed that night. In fact, his scrupulous honesty was a mystery to me. He could never tell our mother a lie without confessing it before bedtime. On the other hand, I was a consummate liar. When Mother sent me in the front door of the Ethridge School with outdated Shirley Temple corkscrew curls, I promptly went out the back door to the bathroom and combed them out. I told her my hair simply wouldn't hold curls, and they "fell out" over the course of the day. Unlike my brother, I felt no compunction about my lies. They slipped off my tongue like oil.

Ultimately, then, our sibling rivalry proved my brother to be the winner. I was cuter and smarter – of that I am quite sure – but, I must admit, he was more honest.

Rest a Spell

1. Briefly share a story of sibling rivalry from your childhood.
2. Is it possible for children growing up in a multichild household to avoid sibling rivalry?
3. Is sibling rivalry more intense between opposite-sex siblings, all-male siblings, or all-female siblings? How do age differences affect rivalry?
4. How did your parents deal with sibling rivalry? If you have children, how do (or did) you contend with it?
5. How do you determine which child is lying and which is telling the truth?
6. What can sibling rivalry lead to in adulthood if not properly controlled?

Walking With the Master

When Nancy Pelosi, the first female speaker of the U.S. House of Representatives, was asked if she could handle the job, she commented, "Having five children in six years is the best training in the world for speaker of the House" (Povich 30). Both a mother and a grandmother, Pelosi knows that groups of adults can often squabble like siblings in a family.

A friend of mine has four daughters, two of whom were essentially the same size in their teenage years. This caused a problem, especially on school mornings, when both of them wanted to wear the same clothes. One morning they were verbally sparring over a particular blouse and were ready to come to blows. Fed up with their constant bickering, their mother took her scissors and, with the wisdom of Solomon, cut the blouse in two and handed each girl half. Needless to say, she cured the problem.

Sibling rivalry has existed ever since God instituted the family unit. The book of Genesis is rife with examples of worst-case scenarios from beginning to end. Peaceful accord has never been a natural endowment in human beings. Every baby comes into the world expecting immediate fulfillment of vital physical and psychological needs, no matter how inconvenient to her parents, and peace does not reign until relief comes. Siblings complicate the problem because they too want attention. Jealousy, blame and strife soon follow. Peaceful compromise and respect for the needs of others are qualities that can be instilled only through teaching, example and experience. Unfortunately, the world is full of old children, some even in their 50s and 60s, who have not internalized these qualities and, therefore, are bad examples.

The first case of sibling rivalry in the Bible is Cain and Abel, who stand as a precursor of the trouble that would ensue between brothers in the generations to follow. Abel's sacrifice was acceptable to God; Cain's was not (Genesis 4:4-5). Much speculation has followed about why God rejected Cain's offering. Through the absence of description – simply stated as "the fruit of the ground" – we can infer that perhaps he did not offer the best of his produce (v. 3). In contrast, Moses' inspired description of Abel's offering says that he "brought of the firstborn of his flock and of their fat" (v. 4). We can see Cain's attitude problem here: not only was he rebellious toward God's commands, but he was also careless and flippant in his worship. When God called attention to his sin, Cain reacted negatively to His rejection and correction. God told him, "If you do what is right, you'll feel good about yourself. If you do what is wrong, then you are letting sin take over your life. Get a grip!" (4:7 paraphrased). We know the tragic end of this story: Abel's murder and Cain's banishment.

Although we do not expect such a violent end in sibling rivalries today, occasionally it does happen. We must teach our children first and foremost to do what is right, then to accept correction and consequences when they do wrong. Finally, we must help them exchange their negative responses, whether anger or self-loathing, to more positive ones. Children who are allowed to be cruel or to accept cruelty as a way of life may be preparing themselves for an adult life filled with physical violence or abuse. Parents must be vigilant in recognizing tendencies toward violence or its result, extreme submissiveness, in each of their children. Thankfully, most of our childhood conflicts today are no more than the natural offshoot of living in constant contact with one another in close quarters. Learning self-control and respect within the family circle will lead to a more productive life in the family, the church and the community at large.

Other sibling rivalries in Genesis were the result of bad decisions and poor parenting. Abram acquiesced to Sarai's request to father the promised son by Hagar instead of waiting on God (16:2), and he sent Hagar and Ishmael away (with God's permission) when Sarah observed the jealousy of Ishmael toward Isaac (21:9-14). In turn, when Isaac and Rebekah had their twin sons, they exacerbated the rivalry of Jacob and Esau by each taking a side (25:27-28). As is often true today, Isaac preferred a more "manly" son who liked the outdoor life and hunting, whereas Rebekah preferred a more creative, sensitive son who could easily become her "mama's boy." Unfortunately, the duplicity of Rebekah and Jacob resulted in the mother and son being separated for life after they stole Esau's blessing from the hands of Isaac (27:1–28:5).

Jacob, in turn, failed to learn from the mistakes of his parents. When he played favorites with the children of Rachel (37:3-4; 42:4), his action resulted in his being deceived as well when his own sons lied about the fate of Joseph (37:31-34). Although the foibles of these generations ultimately made possible the will of God in preparing the way for His Son centuries later, they stand as examples to us of what not to do when bringing up our own children.

Playing favorites will cause resentment and worsen sibling rivalry. Each child deserves to be treated as an individual; one child's talents or interests should not take precedence over those of the other. Avoiding comparison is important. To say, "Look at how many more A's your sister has on her report card than you do," will probably not improve a child's grades. Encouraging that child to compete with himself to improve, followed by praise when he does, avoids the comparison game.

Each child deserves the support of both parents in whatever activities best develop that child's uniqueness, even if the activity is not one that we are personally talented in ourselves. Helping each child find his or her special niche in life to the glory of God is the ultimate goal of good parenting. Too many fathers have pushed their sons to achieve on the athletic field what they themselves could not, no matter the son's talents or interests. Many a son has been berated because of his interest in music, painting or drama. The arts often teach teamwork as effectively as sports, and the skills developed by such activities may prove more useful in the Lord's work than throwing, hitting or kicking a ball. Meanwhile, too many mothers have pushed their daughters to be beauty queens to fulfill their own Cinderella dreams. Being overly focused on physical beauty and on having the latest fashions certainly distracts young girls from the beauty of character emphasized in God's Word (1 Peter 3:3-4). It is easy to fall into the trap of fulfilling our own dreams through our children. This in turn leads to playing favorites when a child is skilled and successful in an activity the parent values, whereas a sibling may be overlooked because of different interests.

Sibling rivalry is inevitable to a greater or lesser degree and is dependent upon gender (whether male-male, female-female, or male-female), the difference in ages, each child's talents and interests (whether shared or different), and the personality of each child. Innate temperament is in our genetic makeup, and self-control must be taught. Jacob and Esau wrestled with each other in the womb (Genesis 25:22), and through digital imaging, we have seen that multiple fetuses interact similarly with each other today (*In the Womb*). Some children simply require more training in anger control and patience, whereas others are more amenable and easygoing. Most important is teaching by example. If children observe their parents behaving angrily, selfishly or impatiently with each other, similar behavior can be expected from the siblings. Conversely, if parents speak in a gentle, quiet voice and demonstrate mutual respect for each other when disagreements arise, children will emulate those behaviors and attitudes.

As Christian parents, we must instill biblical attitudes and actions in our children's lives. Paul says it best: "Let each of you look out not only for his own interests, but also for the interests of others" (Philippians 2:4). For example, children should be encouraged to pray for each other daily; it is difficult to mistreat someone for whom you pray. Siblings also need to learn to be friends with each other as well as with their individual peer groups. Parents can encourage friendship between brothers and sisters by allowing them to make cooperative decisions about activities and whose set of friends outside the family to include. Older children can be given some responsibility in supervising younger siblings but not so much that it can become burdensome. Teaching older children to treat younger ones with kindness is great training for future parenthood. I will never forget the kindness of my brother and his various girlfriends in high school when they allowed me to sit with them at the ballgame or in worship.

Humor, we must remember, goes a long way. After all, a "merry heart does good, like medicine" (Proverbs 17:22). Teasing can be fun, as long as both parties have their chance to be on the giving end and no one's feelings get hurt. It is even healthier when children learn to laugh at themselves. Our sons provided us and each other with many entertaining moments because of the healthy balance in their different talents and interests. The younger was successful in sports in school, but this did not concern his older brother. Able to accept his own lack of athleticism with good humor, our older son bragged about his rare win in a high school varsity tennis match, pausing to add with wry amusement the reason why: his opponent, unfortunately, had only one arm! Our sons' friendship as adults is better today because they were friends as children, able to laugh at each other and themselves.

Psalm 127 tells us how blessed we are to have multiple-child families:

Behold, children are a heritage from the Lord,
The fruit of the womb is a reward.
Like arrows in the hand of a warrior,

So are the children of one's youth.
Happy is the man who has his quiver full of them. (vv. 3-5a)

God has provided us with families in which our children can grow into adult Christians capable of working peaceably in His vineyard. He has placed the responsibility for that growth on parents, in particular fathers (Ephesians 6:4). Ultimately, we are all brothers and sisters of Christ; we are all in the family of God. How well we carry out our roles in our spiritual family is ultimately dependent on the training we receive in our earthly families.

Shod With the Preparation of the Gospel

1. What are some ways that parents can intensify sibling rivalry? Identify mistakes made by parents in Genesis and add others.
2. Discuss the following biblical examples of sibling attitudes and relationships.
   • Exodus 2:2-8; Numbers 12
   • Judges 8:29–9:6   • 2 Samuel 13
   • Luke 15:11-32   • John 7:1-5
3. Is sibling rivalry all bad? What skills can be learned through rivalry that will lead to a successful Christian life?
4. What skills can lead to disastrous results and worldly attitudes?
5. Name some practices that Christian parents can institute to improve sibling relationships.
6. At what age or stage in life should all sibling rivalry cease?

Chapter 6

"For to me, to live is Christ, and to die is gain. ...
For I am hard-pressed between the two, having a desire
to depart and be with Christ, which is far better."
(Philippians 1:21, 23)

Barefoot With Dolly

I first internalized the meaning of death when I was 5 years old and my maternal grandmother, Laura Haggarty, died. I was not as close to Granny as my brother, who was 14 at the time, but I knew her well because she lived with us from time to time. Although I was aware that my parents went to funerals on occasion, I had never been to one, nor had I ever known anyone who had died.

Before I was born, a stroke incapacitated Granny. Although she had taught in a variety of one-room schools for more than 40 years, she could not even say her ABCs. My brother, who was in the primary grades at the time, taught her to read and write again. However, her speech remained slurred, and her steps were unsteady for the rest of her life.

Because Granny had no home of her own in her later years, she lived first with one child and then with another. She was happiest when she stayed at my aunts' and uncles' homes because they allowed her to dip snuff. She was most miserable when she lived with us because my mother denied her this small pleasure in an attempt to improve her health. Mother's intentions were good but fruitless. My earliest memory of Granny was when my mother fussed at her for spitting her illicit contraband, smuggled in by her friend Clara, on the floor between the wall and her bed where she hoped Mother would not find it.

We were at the movies when Granny died. Aunt Billie was keeping her at the time, and we left immediately for her house, where Granny lay still and silent in her bed. My aunt had heard the "death rattle" in her mother's throat and had rushed from her kitchen to the bedroom only to find Granny already gone. The doctor arrived after we did, pronounced her dead, and completed a death certificate. The hearse came to transport her body to the funeral home.

The permanence of death was a new idea to me. After all, I had already heard the tale about my great-grandfather Haggarty who was placed on a cooling board in the parlor of his home after he died. He had cancer of the mouth from a Minié ball that struck his face during the Civil War. As was the custom in the days before funeral homes, the family gathered around the body while the coffin was being constructed. Imagine their surprise when he suddenly sat up and demanded to know what was going on. This family story and movies like *The Ghost and Mrs. Muir* starring Rex Harrison and Gene Tierney kept me from being too concerned about the finality of death.

North Funeral Home was in charge of Granny's service. Her casket, covered in a gray, flocked material over pine, was situated at one end of a room doubled in size by an open wooden bifold door between it and an identical room. The dark pine door facings and baseboards contrasted sharply with the white, pulled-plaster walls and ceilings, tinted pink by two globular floor lamps that softened the whole scene in a comforting way. We sat in wooden folding chairs that felt hard and cold against the backs of my legs underneath the full skirt of my short dress. I shut out the emotional scene around me by staring at the walls and ceiling and imagining scenes and figures in the patterns of the pulled plaster.

I wanted to ask questions, but knew better than to disturb my distraught mother. She was an audible mourner, seemingly beyond the comfort offered by my dad who hovered nearby. Her emotions, however, quickly morphed from grief to anger when Clara arrived to offer her condolences; Mother blamed her for Granny's death because of the snuff Clara had brought her.

No one paid any attention to me, so I crept up to the casket alone. Granny was dressed in a deep burgundy dress, and on her shoulder was pinned an orchid with a rosy throat bought as a tribute by my mother. I was more intrigued, however, with the pink net veil that was draped over the open half-lid of the casket at the back to cascade over the front side, completely covering Granny's face and upper torso. This veil's purpose puzzled me at the time, but I can think of two possible functions. One not-so-pleasant use could have been to keep flies away from the body. North Funeral Home did not have air conditioning in those days, and mourners were kept cool through screened doors and windows, supplemented by handheld fans on sticks advertising the funeral business. However, Granny died in the winter, so the other purpose is more likely: the pink net obscured the darkness of her face since she had requested not to be embalmed.

I saw that veil separating her from those gathered around, and I knew she would not rise up and demand to know what was going on like her father-in-law years before. The pink veil could soften the mask of death as it rested on her face, and the pink lights could wrap the mourners in the warm comfort associated with a mother's womb, but the irrevocable nature of death was a cold reality that demanded acceptance. Perhaps I accepted it better than my mother, who was traumatized again a few years later when we discovered that Granny's grave had fallen in as her casket and its contents returned to the earth from whence it came.

Rest a Spell

1. What is your first memory of death? Were you curious? Frightened?
2. What are some funeral customs that have disappeared during your lifetime? What new customs have come into vogue?
3. What are the most comforting words we can say to the person who has lost someone dear to them? What should we avoid saying?
4. Why do we insist on using euphemisms for death, e.g. "no longer with us" or "she passed away"?
5. We are taught in the Bible that death should be a time of celebration for a child of God. How can we celebrate at such a sorrowful time?
6. Have you planned your funeral? What are some requests that you would make? What do you not want to happen at your funeral?

Walking With the Master

While teaching a Bible school class of kindergarteners, the teacher asked a series of questions about getting to heaven. "If I sell my car and house and give all my money to the poor, will that get me to heaven?" In unison, the children shouted, "No!" "What if I clean the church building, carry food to the sick folks, and attend the ladies Bible class? Will that get me to heaven?" Again the children yelled, "No!" She smiled. They were getting the point of her lesson. "What if I am kind to animals and recycle my cola cans?" Again they answered no. "So," she asked, "how do I get to heaven?" One child raised his hand. "You gotta be dead!" he said.

Children are sometimes more pragmatic than we adults are, especially when it comes to the subject of death. Like the pink veil masking Granny's face, we want to separate ourselves from the reality of death – especially our own – by softening its features with euphemisms, grim humor and denial. We use terms like "passed away," "cashed out," "bought the farm," and "kicked the bucket" instead of died. Even the Bible uses the terms "asleep" (Psalm 13:3; Acts 7:60) and "gave up the ghost" (Job 11:20; Acts 5:5 KJV) as euphemisms for dying. Although there is some truth in many of these substitutions, they actually help us avoid the finality we associate with the word "dead."

We also laugh about our impending demise. I gave a friend of mine a pillow with the motto, "Diet. Exercise. Die anyway!" A favorite bumper sticker says, "Don't take life so seriously. You won't get out of it alive." Basically though, we try to avoid thinking about our own death by shutting it out of our daily consciousness. Our Scarlett O'Hara approach of "I'll think about it tomorrow" works well until we face a medical crisis or someone our age dies. We are forced then, at least briefly, to face our own mortality and the inevitable end. In the words of George Bernard Shaw, "The statistics on death are quite impressive – one out of one people die" ("Death" 137).

Two qualities make death a scary proposition. First is the unknown. Unlike a trip to a foreign country to which we have never been, we cannot read a travel book or go on the Internet for pictures of our destination. Neither can we interview someone who has been there before us. We can't even set a timetable for leaving or plan an itinerary. It is possible that we may sleep through the whole trip. Most importantly, a passport will be unnecessary because we will never return from this journey. Second and even more frightening is that we have to travel alone: no husband, no family or no friends to accompany us; hold our hand along the way; or help us embark. We will even have to leave all our baggage behind, including those possessions we find most comforting. Yes, death is scary. No wonder it is often pictured as the grim reaper in a hooded, black robe with a menacing sickle in hand.

What we know, or think we know, about life after death has been affected to a large degree by our culture. Music, literature and visual arts shape our perceptions of the strange, the mysterious or the unseen and often promote questionable beliefs. For example, songs like "Holes in the Floor of Heaven" (music and lyrics by Billy Kirsch and Steve Wariner) comfort us by telling us that Grandma is up in heaven watching over us. Meanwhile, books like *90 Minutes in Heaven: A True Story of Death and Life* by Don Piper describe personal out-of-body experiences. Culture also affects the words and images we choose.

Even the biblical accounts of the afterlife use the proper names of ancient Greek mythology – Hades, Paradise and Tartarus – to describe the dwelling places of the dead. Over the centuries, the works of poets like John Milton, a Puritan, and the paintings of artists like Michelangelo and Leonardo da Vinci, both of whom were influenced by Catholic theology, have shaped how we view heaven and hell, God and Satan, and angels and demons. The realm of the spiritual depends very much on the language and images of the temporal. It is difficult for us to separate fact from fiction; therefore, how much more frightening it is to "shuffle off this mortal coil" (*Hamlet* 3.1.68) when the mortal is all our senses have ever known.

How then must we who are Christians face our own death? First, we must go to the Book. We can be comforted by the brief scriptures telling us about the afterlife, but more importantly, we can begin applying the numerous scriptures that advise us about how to prepare ourselves spiritually for death. In addition, we can demonstrate our faith in God by setting our temporal affairs in order to make the transition as easy as possible for those we leave behind. Ultimately, these steps require us to face the fact that death is a natural part of living. Thoughts of death for the Christian should not be painful or depressing. Like Paul, we need to be able to say, "For to me, to live is Christ, and to die is gain. ... For I am hard-pressed between the two, having a desire to depart and be with Christ, which is far better" (Philippians 1:21, 23).

The Bible is our only factual source of information about death and the afterlife. Even it is silent about many aspects of the hereafter, leaving us to speculate about what will happen immediately after we die. Although some of us may have experienced puzzling events in our lives, such as the "tunnel" so often described by those who have been resuscitated, we should examine the Scriptures to see if these out-of-the-ordinary experiences fit within the context of the inspired Word. If they fall outside the framework established by the Bible, then obviously they are false, counterfeited by Satan to confuse and deceive us.

We know that no matter how much we desire it, we cannot return to live on this earth once we die. Ecclesiastes tells us that our bodies will go back to the dust and our spirits "will return to God" (12:7). David in Psalm 31:5 says, "Into Your hand I commit my spirit," words repeated by Christ on the cross (Luke 23:46) just before He "yielded up His spirit" (Matthew 27:50). Similarly, Stephen said, "Lord Jesus, receive my spirit" as he died (Acts 7:59). Eastern religions promote reincarnation, and many people who profess to follow Christ have infused this false doctrine into their personal beliefs. Christ, instead, promises a resurrection in an eternal, incorruptible body in a spiritual place called heaven where "there shall be no more death, nor sorrow, nor crying" nor pain (Revelation 21:4). Why would we want our spirit to return to earth in another body made of corruptible clay, only to die again, when we can have an incorruptible, spiritual body in such a wonderful place as heaven?

The Bible offers us much more through the doctrine of resurrection than any Eastern religious philosophy can. "Death is swallowed up in victory" through the death, burial and resurrection of Christ (1 Corinthians 15:54-57). This is the victory we acknowledge, reenact and participate in through the act of baptism:

> Or do you not know that as many of us as were baptized into Christ Jesus were baptized into His death? Therefore we were buried with Him through baptism into death, that just

as Christ was raised from the dead by the glory of the Father, even so we also should walk in newness of life. For if we have been united together in the likeness of His death, certainly we also shall be in the likeness of His resurrection, knowing this, that our old man was crucified with Him, that the body of sin might be done away with, that we should no longer be slaves of sin. (Romans 6:3-6)

Our old sinful way of living is crucified (dies) and is buried through our baptism into Christ, and we rise to a new life as we are resurrected from the water, having put Him on to wear His name – Christian (Galatians 3:27; Acts 11:26). In the same way our old sinful mortal body will die and be buried whereas our "inward man [which] is being renewed day by day" (2 Corinthians 4:16) will be resurrected to live eternally with Christ.

The resurrection of the dead, however, will not occur until Christ's second coming. Peter says we have no idea when this day will occur (2 Peter 3:10), but God has already set the time (Acts 17:31). All material things – the universe, the earth and the works of mankind – will be burned up (2 Peter 3:10). Nothing will be left but what is eternal, which includes our souls. It will be a sad and fearful day for those who have not confessed Christ as Lord before death because they will surely do so on that day, although it will be too late (Romans 14:10-11). For the faithful Christian, however, the day will be a glorious one because the promise of being resurrected from the dead "to an inheritance incorruptible and undefiled and that does not fade away" will have finally come true (1 Peter 1:3-4). Heaven, so vividly described by John in Revelation 21, will become the eternal home of the faithful.

The question still remains, however, about our dwelling place if we die before Christ's second coming. Although several people – including Lazarus, the brother of Mary and Martha; Jairus' daughter; and the son of the widow of Nain – died and were raised from the dead, the Bible does not record what they said about their time out of body. Perhaps their memories were erased like most of our dreams, or perhaps they were unconscious while absent; the Preacher in Ecclesiastes says "the dead know nothing" (9:5). Paul tells about being "caught up into Paradise" and hearing "inexpressible words, which it is not lawful for a man to utter" (2 Corinthians 12:2-6), so perhaps they were not permitted to tell about their sojourn.

Despite their silence on the subject, other references give us a general idea, especially the story about the beggar Lazarus and the rich man in hades (Luke 16:19-31). Divergent opinions about whether this story is a parable or a real event are inconsequential. If a parable, it uses truth as an analogy for a spiritual lesson; if a real event, then the story stands on its own merits. Both men are in hades, the waiting place for the dead; Christ was also briefly in Paradise (Luke 23:43) and, at the same time, hades (Acts 2:31). Lazarus is in "Abraham's bosom," a metaphor for Paradise, and the rich man is across a great gulf in a place of torment, referred to with the Greek word *tartarus* in 2 Peter 2:4. Depending on which translation you read, Peter describes tartarus as "gloomy dungeons" (NIV), "pits of darkness" (ASV), or "chains of darkness" (NKJV). Lazarus, Abraham and the rich man retain their identities; they are recognizable and recognized (Luke 16:23). This is also true of Samuel who was called back from the dead by a medium (1 Samuel 28:12-15) and Moses and Elijah at the transfiguration of Christ (Matthew 17:3-5). The conversation between the rich man and Abraham implies consciousness within the realm of hades but not necessarily consciousness of what is happening on earth: more than likely, the rich man was aware of the lifestyle of his brothers before his death.

Obviously, from the moment of death until the resurrection, we know where we are going to end up – with the sheep or with the goats (Matthew 25:32). The Bible does not support the false doctrine of purgatory; after death neither we nor our loved ones can pray or pay our way from one side of the gulf to the other. We will gather "before the judgment seat of Christ" and be evaluated "according to what [we have] done, whether good or bad" (2 Corinthians 5:10). Our formal sentencing will be based on whether our name appears in the "Lamb's Book of Life" (Revelation 21:27).

For every good, there is an opposing evil; where there is a heaven, there is also a hell. Both are real. Descriptions of hell are as vivid as those of heaven. Although heaven is described as "the great city, the holy Jerusalem" (Revelation 21:10), hell is described as "Gehenna," a polluted refuse heap where toxic waste burned continuously outside the earthly city of Jerusalem. The fires of the eternal hell "shall never be quenched" (Mark 9:43-48) and will be peopled with all kinds of unpleasant company: "the cowardly, unbelieving, abominable, murderers, sexually immoral, sorcerers, idolaters, and all liars" (Revelation 21:8), as well as the devil and his wicked angels (Matthew 25:41) – certainly not pleasant company to keep for all eternity.

We should live, then, in such a way that heaven will be our eternal destination. As children of God and sisters to Christ, we can be assured that God's grace is bountiful, easily tapped into with confession and continuous prayer. Christ serves as our mediator (1 Timothy 2:5) and pleads our case. For that reason, we should not veil the reality of death nor fear it. After all, it is only a temporary separation from our loved ones. Instead, our death should be approached as William Cullen Bryant describes it in his classic poem "Thanatopsis":

> So live that when thy summons comes to join
> The innumerable caravan, that moves
> To the pale realms of shade, where each shall take
> His chamber in the silent halls of death,
> Thou go not, like the quarry-slave at night,
> Scourged to his dungeon, but sustain'd and sooth'd
> By an unfaltering trust, approach thy grave,
> Like one who wraps the drapery of his couch
> About him, and lies down to pleasant dreams. (675)

Shod With the Preparation of the Gospel

1. Read the description of heaven in Revelation 21. Why did the revelator choose the image of a city to describe heaven? (Research the desirability of city life as opposed to rural living in the Holy Land.)
2. Is this image as effective today as it was in Bible times? Why or why not? If you were choosing a temporal location as an analogy for heaven, where or what would you choose?
3. Why do preachers seemingly avoid sermons on hell today? Is teaching about hell necessary?
4. What are some things that you can do to "set your house in order" for your heirs? If you have been involved in settling an estate, share your experiences and make suggestions for others who will face the task.

5. What kind of legacy should we leave behind for our children, grand-children and others?
6. What is the best thing that can be said about us after we die?

Chapter 7

SUPERSTITIONS

*"But reject profane and old wives' fables,
and exercise yourself toward godliness."
(1 Timothy 4:7)*

Barefoot With Dolly

My mother's family was rife with superstition and folklore. When the painting hanging above the buffet in our dining room fell from its nail three days before Granny died, it was absolute proof to me that all our family superstitions were true.

We not only told ghost stories and strange tales, but we also performed all kinds of good luck/bad luck rituals to keep us safe. I have never in my life put my left shoe on before my right. Mother taught me as a child it was bad luck, and old habits die hard. If we dropped a fork at the table, we threw salt over our shoulder. Whatever door of a house we entered, we had to exit by the same door. We treated ladybugs with great respect because they brought good luck. And I did not learn to whistle because "whistling girls and crowing hens always come to some bad end."

My Aunt Alice, not blood kin because she was married to my mother's brother, was a fortune teller of sorts. She could read the designs left in the coffee dregs in a china cup after rotating the cup on its saucer nine times. If she saw white, it frightened her because it could mean either a wedding or a death. The last time she read the coffee grounds she saw white, and her own baby was stillborn. She thought it was God's punishment for looking into the future, and she vowed never to do it again.

The most fascinating superstitions for me had to do with getting married. All those movies I watched growing up gave me romantic notions, and I was truly in love with love, having an infatuation with a new boyfriend every week. I could hardly wait to find out whom I would marry. One superstition involved swallowing a thimbleful of salt and going backwards to bed. Supposedly, a girl would dream that her future husband gave her a drink during the night. I tried this once – only to be strangled by the salt and having to get my own drink. Another superstition involved the number of years until getting married. I would pull a hair from my head and loop it through a ring, then suspend the ring above a glass two-thirds full of water. Mysteriously, the ring would begin to swing. The number of times it tapped the edges of the glass was the number of years until I would get married. Unfortunately, I did this so many times that the number of taps varied, and I could not get a clear answer.

My granny had participated in a "dumb supper" in her youth, but I was never brave enough or had the resources to throw one. Although Granny's dumb supper had failed, I felt sure that if I could take part in one, I could find out who my future husband would be. As Granny's story went, she and her friends gathered at a house where they prepared nine different dishes while walking backwards. All of this was accomplished silently because one spoken word could interrupt the spell. They sat at the table, leaving a space for their future husbands (or their spirits) to sit down beside them. If a girl was so unfortunate as to have a coffin sit down by her, she would end up an old maid.

On this occasion, the wind began to howl. The girls heard horses galloping up to the porch, saddles creaking as the men alit, and footsteps striding through the dogtrot. At this moment Granny's younger brother John, the only male present, picked up a slab of meat, threw it across the room, and with a few unrepeatable words broke the spell. Granny had to take a thimbleful of salt to dream about the outcome that she said all came true.

Other than marriage, death was the other life event most covered by superstitions. We believed in ghosts. We did not step on graves. My Aunt Dixie, who lived in the country and had no phone, was packed and ready when we went to tell her about Granny's passing. She said that she had sensed her mother's death. Granny's rocking chair even rocked by itself one time, and Mother said she woke to find Granny's ghost standing at the foot of her bed.

The picture really did fall off the wall three nights before Granny died. It was a superstition like the one about a clock stopping when someone dies, immortalized in a popular song of that day, "My Grandfather's Clock." I remember how we all sat up in bed, not knowing what the crash was. We followed my dad with his flashlight to the dining room where the painting, a favorite of Granny's, rested on the buffet while leaning against the wall. It sat there untouched for weeks after Granny's funeral.

Although I find this merely coincidental now, I am still puzzled by a strange, deeply personal event – a disturbing dream I had the night before a life-changing automobile accident when I was 15. I dreamed that I got in a casket and tried it on for size. It wasn't mine; it didn't fit. The next day, if a man whose name I do not know had not used his carjack to release my neck from the vice formed by the steering wheel and the top brace of our flipped car, I would have died. The casket would have fit.

Rest a Spell

1. What good luck/bad luck superstitions did you follow when you were growing up? Do these rituals still affect your behavior today?
2. Do you avoid opening an umbrella inside? Do you avoid walking under ladders? Do you notice whether a cat that crosses in front of your car is black? Do you take special notice that it is Friday the 13th? Do you read your horoscope – just for fun?
3. Do you know of someone who follows a particular ritual or who carries something special when performing (i.e., sports, speaking, acting)? What are some items that people think of as good luck charms?
4. Should children read or view *The Wizard of Oz* or the Harry Potter series? How much "magic" is too much?
5. Why are we so fascinated with ghost stories?

Walking With the Master

A prospective skydiver who was taking parachute training kept asking the instructor questions about the impending first jump. "And what happens if both the main chute and the spare chute don't open?" he queried nervously. The instructor replied, "That, young man, is what is known as jumping to a conclusion."

Jumping to a conclusion is what we all do when we behave in a certain way based on a superstitious belief. At some time in the past, someone has made a faulty connection between cause and effect, leading us to think that two events are related when actually they are not. In fact, one definition of superstition is "a belief that some action or circumstance not logically related to a course of events influences its outcome" ("Superstition," *American*). Many of these fallacious beliefs are merely folklore, passed down from generation to generation in our families and our culture. Although we may no longer believe in the truth of the superstition, it still affects our behavior because we are cognizant of its existence, and old habits die hard. Some rituals, such as always putting on the same shoe first or turning around in the reverse direction to "unwind" ourselves, may be mild forms of obsessive-compulsive disorder. Whether or not we are plagued by OCD, we humans are very ritualistic and tradition bound. Just check to see how many worshipers sit in the same seat every service!

The fallacy of questionable cause underlies most of our good luck/bad luck superstitions. Rhymes such as "step on a crack, break your mother's back" and "an apple a day keeps the doctor away" are among the more reasonable sayings. After all, we might fall on uneven ground, and fruit is nutritious. A more irrational rhyme, however, connects the day of our birth with our personality: "Monday's child is fair of face, Tuesday's child is full of grace. ..." We have been brought up hearing that breaking a mirror will result in seven years of bad luck, that we must blow out all the candles on a birthday cake for a wish to come true, and that we should get in and out of a bed on the same side. Many superstitions are meant to control behavior. For example, we tell our children that if they don't eat the crust of their bread, they won't be able to whistle.

• **Luck.** Of all life's rituals, none is more filled with superstition than a wedding. In addition to wearing a veil and a white dress, a bride wants to carry "something old, something new, something borrowed, something blue" for good luck. At the same time, her desire for a plethora of photographs may prompt her to ignore the possibility of bad luck if her groom sees her before the ceremony. We both ignore and invent superstitions to suit our fancy. After all, don't we believe nowadays that it will rain if we wash the family car?

Luck is so much a feature of our thinking that it permeates our entire society. Take, for example, *paraskavedekatriaphobia*, the fear of Friday the 13th. Although we are supposedly less paranoid than we were in 1987, the *Smithsonian* magazine reported then that this superstitious fear caused "absenteeism, travel cancellations, and other hits to commerce in general" resulting in the loss of $1 billion to our economy. Similarly, *triskaidekaphobia*, the fear of the number 13, affects some buildings, causing architects to omit the 13th floor in numbering (although logically the 14th floor is still the 13th) and to skip 13 in room numbers (Brus). Although more modern buildings do not give credence to this superstition, the number 666 has evoked a similar phobia; it is now the room number more often omitted.

The lyrics of a favorite song often sung by Buck Owens and Roy Clark on the old TV show *Hee Haw* featured the line, "If it weren't for bad luck, I'd have no luck at all." Unfortunately, for those people who attribute all the potholes in life's road to luck, this may be true. Ralph Waldo Emerson once said, "Shallow men believe in luck. Strong men believe in cause and effect" (Emerson).

In his book *The Luck Factor*, Richard Wiseman, head of the psychology research department at the University of Hertfordshire in England, points out that the difference in people who consider themselves lucky and those who see themselves as unlucky has much to do with their reactions to the vicissitudes of life. Positive thinkers are more flexible in taking advantage of opportunities that force them to think and act outside their comfort zone. These so-called lucky people also make the best of an unpleasant situation by searching for an extraneous good result that may come out of the bad. Wiseman suggests four principles for being lucky: (1) "Maximize chance opportunities"; (2) "Listen to your lucky hunches"; (3) "Expect good fortune"; and (4) "Turn bad luck into good" (qtd. in Pink).

Christians, however, do not need a psychologist to know that there are better principles to apply. God is in charge of all outcomes: "The lot is cast into the lap, But its every decision is from the Lord" (Proverbs 16:33). Meanwhile, we are taught to maximize our opportunities and be ready. Paul says, "Therefore, as we have opportunity, let us do good to all, especially to those who are of the household of faith" (Galatians 6:10), and "Be wise in the way you act toward outsiders; make the most of every opportunity" (Colossians 4:5 NIV). Instead of listening to lucky hunches, we are taught to "pray without ceasing" (1 Thessalonians 5:17) and to "be anxious for nothing, but in everything by prayer and supplication, with thanksgiving, let your requests be made known to God" (Philippians 4:6). Rather than seeking good fortune, we expect that "all things work together for good to those who love God" (Romans 8:28) because we know that "If God is for us, who can be against us?" (v. 31). By expecting the best, no matter the outcome, we can turn what seems bad into good like Paul who said, "I can do all things through Christ who strengthens me" (Philippians 4:13). Luck is trumped by the love of God. Therefore, Christians need to be wary of saying "I was lucky" or "I was fortunate"; rather, let us give credit where it is due and say, "I was blessed."

• **Idol Worship.** A second definition of superstition is "any belief, practice, or rite unreasoningly upheld by faith in magic, chance or dogma" ("Superstition," *American*). The use of the word "dogma" in this secular source suggests that religion is superstition, a position held by atheistic groups who support naturalism, a dogma in itself that denies the existence of all spiritual beings and spiritual realms (Ingersoll). Truly any belief, including naturalism, is superstitious if it is not based on the inerrant Word of God. In contrast, a distinctly religious definition of superstition is given by *The Catholic Encyclopedia*: "Observances added on to prescribed or established worship" or a "vice opposed to religion by way of excess; not because in the worship of God it does more than true religion, but because it offers divine worship to beings other than God or offers worship to God in an improper manner" ("Superstition"). Although this definition actually encompasses all the varieties of superstition, it places emphasis on adding our own human twist to worship practices commanded by God. This definition would perhaps cover worshiping an image of Jesus envisioned in smudges on a refrigerator or the Virgin Mary seen on a rock, both touted as miraculous events by naive believers in the late 1990s and early 2000s. In light of New Testament Christianity, the *Catholic Encyclopedia* definition doesn't go far enough. It should also cover worshiping before statues or praying to particular saints who are "beings other than God" not described or prescribed in the first-century church.

Indeed, idol worship is listed in the Ten Commandments and condemned more often than any other sin throughout the Scriptures (Exodus 20:3-4). Idolatry was the primary reason that the Israelites were forbidden to marry or live among foreigners. For example, despite God's warning through his prophet Jeremiah, a defiant remnant of Judeans under the leadership of Johanan went to live in lower Egypt because they feared the Chaldeans. There the women, with their husbands' permission, burned incense, offered drink offerings and cakes to the queen of heaven (the moon) in worship. As prophesied by Jeremiah, they were destroyed along with the Egyptians (Jeremiah 42–44).

Attaching special importance to religious objects is also condemned by Scripture. During the last days of Eli as high priest, the Israelites brought the ark of the covenant into their camp after being defeated by the Philistines. They thought its presence would bring them victory despite their disobedience to God. When the Israelites shouted at the ark's arrival, the Philistines were afraid because they too thought that God had appeared. However, the presence of the ark and their fear only served to make the Philistines fight harder. As a result, they won a great battle over the Israelites and captured the ark (1 Samuel 4:1-11).

During Christ's ministry, the scribes and Pharisees were swearing by the temple gold and the altar and giving a superstitious importance to these items (Matthew 23:16-22). Their religious practices were as vain as those of the Athenians whom Paul told, "God, who made the world and everything in it, since He is Lord of heaven and earth, does not dwell in temples made with hands. Nor is He worshiped with men's hands" (Acts 17:24-25).

Lest our worship, too, become vain, let us be vigilant in separating tradition from true worship. Traditions become superstitions when material objects and rituals become as important as the avenues of worship commanded by God. Churches have split over such inconsequential matters as placing a cloth on the communion table, replacing a single piece of communion bread with many pieces, or removing the pulpit from the stage. We forget that much of what we physically place in a church building (pews, pulpit, hymnals) are traditions that are handed down through previous generations of Protestants who, in turn, incorporated much of what had preceded them as part of the Catholic tradition. For example, the pulpit was originally an ambo with a shape and height that helped amplify a priest's discourse in a cathedral before the invention of electricity and microphones. All of these items are expediencies that were not available to the New Testament church that met in homes. To attach significance to any of these material objects in worship constitutes superstition.

• **Fortune Telling.** Extraneous also to prescribed worship are practices that predict the future, such as fortune telling, palm and tarot card readings, and horoscopes. Ezekiel told God's people to "no longer envision futility nor practice divination" (13:23). In the Bible, divination or foretelling the future is most often associated with the work of demons. In Philippi, Paul incensed the owners of a slave girl who could tell fortunes when he cast out the demon that possessed her, thus removing their source of income (Acts 16:16-20).

• **Dreams.** Even dreams are suspect. Psychologists have had little success in making sense of the dream world we all experience while sleeping. According to Raymond Lloyd Richmond, Ph.D. in clinical psychology, many dreams that disturb us appear in our subconscious for various reason: to give us unconscious advice; to admonish us based on our guilt; to express repressed trauma; or to give psychic premonitions, a rare phenomenon ("Guide"). Rather than apply the philosophy of psychoanalysts, however, it is always wise for the Christian to question the source of any dream that seems to give us advice or to foretell an event: is it from God or from the devil? We are told that "Satan transforms himself into an angel of light" (2 Corinthians 11:14). Certainly we must be wary of formulating or changing our plans based on dreams.

Although Joseph had prophetic dreams that came from God, the Israelites were later commanded to beware of a "dreamer of dreams" even if "he gives you a sign or a wonder, and the sign or the wonder comes to pass." The true test of such a prophet could be better found in his words: he should be put to death if he said to follow after other gods (Deuteronomy 13:1-5).

Some events in life cannot be logically explained. Perhaps it is best for us to keep such mystifying incidents private rather than try to rationalize or justify them. Shakespeare's Hamlet says, "There are more things in heaven and earth, Horatio, Than are dreamt of in your philosophy" (*Hamlet* 1.5.167-68).

• **Angels and Demons.** We know that angels and demons exist, but we do not know when or how much they influence our lives today. During the time that Jesus lived on earth, demons appear to have been more prevalent, allowing Him to demonstrate not only His divinity but also His power over them. As for angels, the Hebrews writer says, "Do not forget to entertain strangers, for by so doing some have unwittingly entertained angels" (13:2), and he asks, "Are [angels] not all ministering spirits sent forth to minister for those who will inherit salvation?" (1:14).

• **Ghosts.** Spirits of those who have preceded us to hades (Luke 16:22-23), however, are another matter altogether. Samuel appeared to Saul, but it was not by the power of the medium. Her frightened reaction to the success of her séance demonstrates that she had never before been so successful (1 Samuel 28:3-25). Moses and Elijah appeared with the transfigured Christ before Peter, James and John (Matthew 17:1-3), but this special event served to demonstrate the superiority of the Savior. Dead saints were resurrected at the time of Christ's death on the cross and appeared to many in Jerusalem, but whether they remained alive on earth in their bodies for any length of time is not revealed (Matthew 27:52-53). Obviously in the story of the rich man and Lazarus, special permission is necessary for a spirit to be authorized to return to earth (Luke 16:27-28). Ghostly emanations today may be no more than an active imagination under duress from the death of a loved one or from some other stressful event, or they may be the work of the devil.

• **The Occult.** As a society we are fascinated by the weird, the strange, the bizarre. Talented writers like Stephen King continue to write best sellers, and the movies based on these literary works frighten us with images of demons, witches and the occult. Movies in the horror genre, such as *The Omen, The Exorcist* and *Carrie*, are especially popular with young people who are fascinated by devil worship and occult practices. We need to take special care to separate fiction from nonfiction and to err on the side of caution in what we let our children view and read. In doing so, we will be taking to heart Paul's instructions to "reject profane and old wives' fables, and exercise yourself toward godliness" (1 Timothy 4:7).

Shod With the Preparation of the Gospel

1. Why do definitions of "superstition" vary so much? How do you decide what is superstitious and what is not?
2. What is the difference in a tradition and a superstition? What are some objects, rituals and beliefs associated with religion that Christians have held on to superstitiously?
3. Should Christians wear a cross as jewelry? Why or why not?
4. In recent years churches have avoided traditional Halloween parties by planning alternative activities. Discuss this change, why it has occurred, and what activities work best in this situation.
5. Has praying before a sporting event become a superstition? Does God take sides when two opposing teams pray to win? Is it wrong to pray for victory in sporting events?
6. Why is it important for us to verbalize publicly that we are blessed rather than that we are subject to good fortune?

Chapter 8

Victory for VICTIMS

"If God is for us, who can be against us?"
(Romans 8:31)

Barefoot With Dolly

Because I was a precocious child, my mother started my education before I reached school age. She bought copies of the school reading texts at the superintendent's office and read aloud to me while placing her finger under each word. I may have read the first books simply through memorization, but I did learn to read. In fact I had read through the fourth grade reader by the time I was 6, ready to start to school. Because of my mother's effective teaching, I started school in the second grade, making me the youngest student in the class. I am sure the other students were more than a little resentful that I could begin one grade later than they had.

Our teacher was Miss Ruby, a giant of a woman who stood at 6 feet 1 inch with a body to match her frame. Needless to say, to a second grader she was a bit overwhelming. She was loving and kind but, at the same time, a stern disciplinarian. In fact, she awed us so much that she could safely leave us unsupervised for the last hour of school while she coached basketball in the gym. We knew better than to mess with Miss Ruby. Her nephew Mike, who was quite the cowboy, laid his lariat at the screen door of the room hoping to rope her as she came in. He was invited to a private meeting with her paddle in the cloakroom. All of us met her paddle one day when she returned to find us out of our seats. She simply went up and down the rows giving each one a swat.

Miss Ruby moved with my class from first through third grade. She was an excellent teacher who used spelling and math bees to make our learning more competitive. I doubt these bees were much fun for some kids, but I enjoyed them even though I rarely won. Spelling and math were two of my weaker subjects. My strongest talent, of course, was in reading, but having completed all the readers before entering school made no difference in my instruction. I read the same books over again with the rest of the class. My weakest subjects, handwriting and art, were related to my poor eye-hand coordination. Cursive writing, when introduced in fourth grade, was my bane; and art, although enjoyable, was messy at best. Being younger and a little less mature than the other students had its problems.

These troubles extended to the playground as well. The class bully – at least in my eyes – was Jane. I knew her before I started to school because she pushed all her guests, including me, down in a ditch at her fifth birthday party and truly got a birthday spanking. Jane was both athletic and smart. In races at recess, she always came in first. When playing red rover, her grip was unbreakable. She could climb the jungle gym faster and turn more flips quicker than any other classmate, and no child wanted to be on the popping end of a human whip when Jane was controlling the chain. Even the boys were afraid of her.

Jane seemed to find the most pleasure in tormenting me for my athletic ineptitude. I was the last one picked for relay games and played "it" in tag more often than any of my classmates. I never dodged quickly enough to avoid the ball, and how anyone could hit a softball with a bat was beyond me. As a result, at recess I avoided the more strenuous activities – and Jane – by playing school with quieter children on the gym steps. We advanced up through the grades – and steps – by guessing the hand in which the "teacher" hid a rock. We also jumped rope collectively while counting out, "Cinderella, dressed in yellow, came to town to meet her fellow. How many kisses did he give her? One, two, three ... ." At other times we played store. We pushed boards between the double row of saplings at the back of the playground, gathered up empty cans and boxes, and pretended to sell our merchandise. We also "baptized" each other, but I felt guilty for participating because my mother had told me that was not acceptable play.

Unfortunately in the classroom, I could not avoid Jane's pointed comments about my art projects as compared to hers. These primary grade masterpieces were meant to be gifts for our mothers, who were, of course, our kindest and most appreciative art critics. Our projects included a painted trash can made from a five-gallon green bean can from the cafeteria, a Christmas card picture framed in a jar ring with a pipe cleaner hanger, and an Easter egg bunny with a cotton ball tail. In none of these did I outdo Jane.

I had my moments, though. When we were asked to write poetry, I had a natural gift for rhythm and rhyme – perhaps because I had read all of Robert Louis Stevenson's poems several times over. I could also sing well in music class and was taking piano lessons. In addition, I was quite the actress. In second grade I played the angel who brought the "good tidings of great joy" in my painted cardboard wings covered with shiny flakes of Lux detergent. The next year I was Snow White in "Snow White Goes to PTA."

I can thank Jane for challenging me in the sixth grade because it led to positive consequences. When my art suddenly improved with the maturation of my eye-hand coordination, my report card became her new topic. At the end of one six-weeks period, she bragged, "I have two more A's than you!" Her comment made me angry, but I knew it was my own fault. My study habits always received a grade of C because I was bored with continuous repetition. I really hadn't cared about my grades before that time. However, from the next grading period through the eighth grade, I made straight A's. Jane's bullying was the impetus for positive change. The runt finally outran the bully, as well as the rest of the class.

Rest a Spell

1. Did you have a class bully in elementary school? How did you react to him or her?
2. Was Jane actually a bully, or was she just a strong-willed, talented

student? What is the difference in bullying and competing?

3. What changes have occurred in classroom teaching and behavior management since Dolly's school days? Are those changes for the better?

4. How has recess changed in the last decade or so? How can "free play" be a positive experience for children? Do we over-supervise children at play today?

5. In what ways did you think you were not as talented as others in your class? How did you compensate for your inadequacies?

6. What are some factors that may cause a child, or a grown-up, to bully others?

Walking With the Master

Mark Martin, a seasoned NASCAR driver, lost the 2007 Daytona 500 by 0.020 seconds. His car was in the lead position when a spectacular wreck happened. He could have contested his loss since NASCAR rules state that the running order of cars is frozen when a crash occurs. However, Martin said, "I didn't ask for a win. I asked for a chance to win. I had that chance and I let it slip through my fingers. ... But my heart's not broke. I've had a lot worse happen to me over the years" (Woody 4C). In this age of in-your-face confrontation, it is rare to see someone practice such civility in questionable defeat.

Civility has virtually disappeared and has been replaced by name-calling, disrespect, rudeness and vulgarity – all forms of bullying. Today, bullying is the most common tactic to win at all costs. Bullying can be defined as "the use of fear, manipulation and intimidation to gain power and control" (Reist 52). It is a serious problem in the United States, both in schools and in the workplace. Unfortunately, bullying is a result of a cultural climate of our own making; it is as American as apple pie (Piazza). Today, stepping on the rights of others, spreading rumors and lies about those opposed to our goals, and manipulating cutthroat business deals are acceptable tactics to rise to the top in our society.

The school system in America, as a microcosm of our society, is the perfect medium for breeding young bullies and victims. One-fourth of elementary school children have been, at one time or another, the target of bullying; and 43 percent of middle school and high school students avoid using the school restroom out of fear of harassment and/or assault. Each school year, 3 million incidents of bullying in schools are reported, and estimates say that more than 160,000 children miss school to avoid harassment. In rural areas of the Midwest alone, 90 percent of middle school students and 66 percent of high school students report having been victimized during their years in school. It must be noted, however, that bullying is not just an American phenomenon. It occurs in every Western nation and has accompanied the westernization of Eastern cultures. Japan, in particular, now has a high number of reported incidents of bullying, called *ijime*, in its schools (Smith-Heavenrich).

Our American male children, in particular, are subject to one type of bullying, sexual harassment. This is especially true in rural Southern culture where, as a backlash against the nationwide agenda to accept homosexual lifestyles, any boy who does not fit the artificially imposed masculinity code is subjected to derogatory name-calling that attacks his manhood. GenderPAC's executive director, Riki Wilchins, says that this "boy code" is based on old stereotypes: "Boys need to keep their emotions in check, violence is an acceptable response to emotional upset, [and] self-esteem relies on power" ("Is 'Masculinity' "). This code was so rigid in a high school where I once taught that male athletes who participated in the "less manly" sports of soccer, tennis, golf and even basketball were taunted by their peers as being gay. Certainly, a boy who was "nerdy" or a member of the high school band had no chance of escaping such hazing. Unfortunately, the Christian community can inadvertently support this type of bullying by combining biblical teaching against homosexual practices with non-biblical, hatemongering attitudes that translate for the young into approval of such harassment.

Meanwhile, the apathetic response of many school administrators, teachers and coaches condones bullying as a natural part of life. Turning a blind eye to the situation often leads to more violent acts. For example, the likelihood of a child committing suicide is greater if he or she is a victim of bullying: "Boys who are bullied are four times more likely to be suicidal; girls eight times more likely" (Frieden). Another violent result is murder. In 1998, Kip Kinkel, a teenager living in Springfield, Ore., wrote in his journal, "I hate being laughed at. But they won't laugh after they're scraping parts of their parents, sisters, brothers, and friends from the wall of my hate." He then killed both his parents and shot and injured 25 classmates, and killed two more. Out of 37 school shooting incidents over the last few years, the Secret Service National Threat Assessment Center found that in more than two-thirds of the incidents "the attackers felt persecuted, bullied, threatened, attacked, or injured by others" (Piazza). The violent nature of these tragic events and the weaponry used often overshadow the primary cause. As a result, we add security measures to the physical buildings while continuing to ignore the emotional and social dynamics within the bully/victim relationship.

Although one-third of all bullies are victims themselves, recent research shows that most bullies begin to act aggressively in their preschool years, leading them to the conclusion that aggression is the best solution to conflict. Feeding this attitude is the esteem in which bullies in the middle and high school culture are held, often being considered "cool" while their victims are held in contempt as sissies or weaklings. Although most bullies start off with the same intellectual skills as other students, as they get older they do not perform as well in school and are more apt to experiment with drugs and alcohol and to participate in hazardous activities like speeding and drag racing (Smith-Heavenrich).

Although a smaller percentage of girls are bullies, they can be exceedingly nasty to each other, as depicted in the movie *Mean Girls*. Twenty-five percent of bullies are female, and "cat fights" serve as entertainment in school hallways for enthusiastic onlookers who cheer on the participants. Some girls never outgrow their jealousy and spitefulness as adults, using gossip, insults and lies to make life difficult for others. This tendency was tragically demonstrated by the Missouri mother who pretended to be a teenage boy named Josh to harass 13-year-old Megan Meier on the Internet. When "Josh" cruelly told the young teen that the world would be a better place without her in it, she committed suicide. Although no Missouri laws existed against cyberbullying, the harasser was charged with "one count of conspiracy and three counts of accessing protected computers without authorization" ("Mom").

Overly permissive parents who give in to obnoxious or demanding children are sending them the message that bullying pays off. On the flip side, parents who demand unquestioning obedience, who ridicule their children, or who discipline them out of anger are reinforcing bullying through their poor example. Teaching children how to negotiate peacefully and how to mediate their own disputes are essential tools for both bullies and victims (Smith-Heavenrich). Biblical examples abound: Abraham's peaceful solution to the land dispute with Lot (Genesis 13), Joseph's non-retaliatory attitude toward his brothers (Genesis 42-47), and the resolution of the disagreement between Paul and Barnabas over John Mark (Acts 15:36-41).

Bullying also occurs in adult situations, especially in the workplace. Examples of harassment in the workplace include undermining a more successful co-worker with vicious gossip, ridiculing a co-worker or subordinate publicly, dumping excessive work or unpleasant jobs on subordinates, and threatening loss of job or even violence. The bully often succeeds by poisoning the workplace through suggestion, innuendo and fear. Co-workers will often side with the bully rather than recognize the behavior for what it is. Solidarity of the work force early on helps to combat the situation, but it is often difficult to initiate because individual workers worry that they will be the next target. Bullying takes its toll on employees through anxiety, depression, exhaustion, insecurity, poor concentration and sleeplessness. The results of bullying are costly to corporations. Victims intentionally decrease the quality and quantity of work, take sick leave to avoid being bullied, and ultimately change jobs (Yandrick).

Terrorism is the ultimate form of bullying. Ramming hijacked airplanes into buildings, sending suicide bombers into crowds, broadcasting the execution of innocent people, and exterminating millions of Jews in concentration camps are all bullying at its worst. The nations that attended the Geneva Conventions assembled to prevent such atrocities, but bullies have always ignored rules. In addition, when religious beliefs play a role in the act of bullying, the bully feels justified in his actions.

Bullying, as it occurs in its various forms, is a factor in several incidents in the Bible, often resulting in violence. Joseph was certainly the victim of bullying by his older brothers, who scoffed at his dreams. When they threw him in a pit, he would have died had it not been for the intervention of Reuben. Instead, the brothers sold him into slavery (Genesis 37:18-28).

David was taunted in his youth by Goliath (1 Samuel 17:43) but later played the bully by abusing his position and power as king. David had the innocent Uriah placed at the battlefront to be killed so that he could take Bathsheba as his wife (2 Samuel 11). On another occasion, David's servants were the victims of harassment when he sent them to express his sympathy and kindness to Hanun, the son of King Nahash of Ammon who had recently died. Hanun's advisors, who questioned David's motives, "shaved off half of their beards" and "cut off their garments in the middle, at their buttocks," shaming them (2 Samuel 10:1-5).

The prophet Elisha was also mocked. A gang of young men repeatedly called out to him, "Go up, you baldhead!" Little did they know that Elisha was empowered by God to call down the wrath of two female bears who mauled 42 of them (2 Kings 2:23-24).

Bullying is condemned in the Old Testament. The law given by Moses curses anyone "who treats his father or his mother with contempt," who "makes the blind to wander off the road," or who "perverts the justice due the stranger, the fatherless, and widow" (Deuteronomy 27:16, 18-19). Isaiah condemns those who mock the righteous: "You sons of the sorceress, You offspring of the adulterer and the harlot! whom do you ridicule? Against whom do you make a wide mouth and stick out the tongue?" (57:3-4). Proverbs 24:17-18 even warns against rejoicing when an enemy falls, "Lest the LORD see it, and it displease Him, And He turn away His wrath from him."

Certainly Christians should not bully others, but sometimes they do, even in the church. John, the apostle of love, writes about Diotrephes loving "to have the preeminence" and refusing to have a letter from John read to the church. John also says that Diotrephes "does not receive the brethren and forbids those who wish to, putting them out of the church" (3 John 9-10). We occasionally hear today of similar situations in congregations, especially where no eldership is in place. Without a plurality of elders, it is easy for a bully to lord it over other men of the congregation in business meetings and to make demands based on his own preferences, ideas and traditions. In one such case, an older man in a small rural congregation insists that only the 1611 version of the King James Bible be used and that women wear dresses to every worship and Bible study meeting of the church.

Once such a person has gained power, it is difficult for the preacher or congregation to loosen his grip on the church.

But what about the victims of bullying? If they are God's children, they have victory despite their persecution. David promises in Psalm 37 that "the meek shall inherit the earth" and have peace. He says the Lord laughs at the wicked who "cast down the poor and needy" and "slay those who are of upright conduct" because their own swords will kill them and their bows will be broken (vv. 11-15).

Christ repeats David's words when He says, "Blessed are the meek, For they shall inherit the earth" (Matthew 5:5). Christ Himself is our ultimate example of non-retaliatory response to harassment and abuse. The soldiers mocked Him, spat upon Him and slapped Him as He stood dressed in a scarlet robe and crown of thorns to ridicule His kingship (27:27-30). Christ teaches us to love our enemies, bless those who curse us, do good to those who hate us, and pray for those who spitefully use us and persecute us (5:44). The Hebrews writer reminds us that those who lived before Christ's sacrifice for our sins suffered persecution too but we have received the better promise:

> [Some] were tortured, not accepting deliverance, that they might obtain a better resurrection. Still others had trial of mockings and scourgings, yes, and of chains and imprisonment. They were stoned, they were sawn in two, were tempted, were slain with the sword. They wandered about in sheepskins and goatskins, being destitute, afflicted, tormented – of whom the world was not worthy. They wandered in deserts and mountains, in dens and caves of the earth. And all these, having obtained a good testimony through faith, did not receive the promise, God having provided something better for us, that they should not be made perfect apart from us. (Hebrews 11:35-40)

We should remember that God did not spare His own son. Despite the hardships that come our way, we are the victors because our final reward cannot be taken from us by any bully. After all, "If God is for us, who can be against us?" (Romans 8:31-32).

Rather than being a bully or a victim, we need to practice the civility and kindness exemplified by David in the Old Testament and by Christ in the New. Although David sinned in his actions toward Uriah, he showed kindness toward the only living descendent of Saul – Jonathan's lame son, Mephibosheth. David, in remembrance of his good friend Jonathan, brought Mephibosheth into his home to eat at his table and gave him all the lands and servants that had belonged to Saul (2 Samuel 9:1-13). Christ said that He was sent to "preach the gospel to the poor … , to heal the brokenhearted … , To proclaim liberty to the captives, [to proclaim] recovery of sight to the blind, [and] To set at liberty those who are oppressed" (Luke 4:18). He also taught that "when you give a feast, invite the poor, the maimed, the lame, the blind" (Luke 14:13). Time and again, He demonstrated what He taught by helping those in trouble both physically and spiritually, whether rich or poor.

Being a Christian gives us our identity. Through salvation in Jesus Christ, we can gain the confidence and self-esteem needed to face the bullies in this life. We can say with Paul, "I have learned in whatever state I am, to be content: I know how to be abased, and I know how to abound" (Philippians 4:11-12). What a wonderful attitude to have! No matter how hard life hits us, we can "roll with the punches" and get up off the mat accepting either victory or defeat in this life, knowing that ultimately God will present us the trophy of eternal life in heaven.

Shod With the Preparation of the Gospel

1. Discuss how bullying affects our children in school and suggest some remedies for the problem.
2. How does bullying by males differ from bullying by females?
3. What qualities in a male are manly? What qualities are not? Was Christ manly?
4. What are some ways that we as Christians may inadvertently encourage bullying?
5. How do people today use their religious beliefs to try to bully others?
6. Christ demonstrated kindness and compassion during His ministry on earth. Make a list of specific incidents. Here are some scriptures to get you started: Matthew 9:36; 19:13-15; 20:30-34; Mark 8:22-25; Luke 17:12-18; 19:41-44; John 4:7-26; 11:33-35.

Chapter 9

"There is neither Jew nor Greek, there is neither slave nor free, there is neither male nor female; for you are all one in Christ Jesus." (Galatians 3:28)

Barefoot With Dolly

I grew up going to the movies. As a young child, I can dimly recall the blue velvet curtains at the Princess Theater surrounding the black and gray images that flickered across the small white screen. The Princess, however, was replaced and dwarfed in 1950 by the new Crockett Theater with its 1,100 seats. The Crockett was art deco at its best with glowing circular neon lights between mock Egyptian columns. A painted border of pink and blue circles on a yellow background completed the motif. Two carpeted aisles ran the full length of the theater, illuminated by evenly spaced downlights marking the way for latecomers. Eight rows from the back in the center section was my dad's favorite place – a double-wide theater seat next to the left aisle. My mother sat next to him with me on the inside next to her.

We always arrived early for the movies, partly to watch the intricate opening of the curtains. As the rose-colored velvet travelers slowly gathered outward, the sheer chiffon curtain beneath would rise from the middle to the outer edge in a row of scallops to reveal the huge movie screen. The first image – often the roaring MGM lion – would appear before the curtains had cleared the entire screen. Of course, another reason to arrive early was to catch up on world events on the Movietone News and to enjoy such cartoons as *Tom and Jerry, Heckle and Jeckle, Foghorn Leghorn* and *Bugs Bunny.*

My family would attend the movies one or two times a week and, on rare occasions when a good Western was offered, three times a week. A postcard was mailed to our home by the theater management announcing the next week's schedule. The first film was usually shown on Sunday through Tuesday nights, a second movie played on Wednesday and Thursday nights – unless the first film had an extended run – and the inevitable Western drew less discriminate audiences on Friday and Saturday nights. Films were not rated because all movies were suitable for children. There were no sex scenes or cursing.

My parents' familiarity with this movie house and its owner Mr. Ruhlander as well as his two regular employees, Mrs. Brink and Mr. Burdine, made it the perfect place for me to stay when my mother served as district PTA president. She would attend out-of-county functions to give speeches, and, because she never learned to drive, my dad would accompany her as chauffeur and escort. I would be left in the care of the theater personnel, my surrogate baby sitters, to watch whatever movie was showing. Several times, my mother's destination was far enough away that I would see the movie through twice in one night. On one or two occasions, when my parents were not back by the end of the second showing, Mr. Ruhlander put in the first reel for a third showing while he and Mr. Burdine swept the theater.

I can still remember dramas like *River of No Return, Apache* and *Raintree County*; musicals like *Kiss Me, Kate* and *Seven Brides for Seven Brothers*; and comedy series that featured Ma and Pa Kettle and Francis the talking mule. During one week when my mother spoke on three consecutive nights, I saw *The Mississippi Gambler* with Tyrone Power and Piper Laurie six-and-a-half times and could even quote several lines. I knew all the movie stars and planned to be an actress when I grew up. I was in love at various times with many of the male stars like Sal Mineo and Tab Hunter. Rock Hudson was the handsomest man alive, in my opinion, and I planned to marry him if he would wait for me to grow up. Of course, I didn't know what these men were like in real life.

The Crockett Theater became my favorite place away from home, but one area of it was forbidden. A huge balcony rested above the lobby, extending out over the back four rows of seats below. In the balcony were the projection booth and about 200 seats. Staircases, carpeted in the same floral design as the first floor, led upward on either side of the area for smokers between the lobby and seating area. The stairs beckoned me upward to this forbidden area, but they were blocked by elaborately decorated aluminum gates. Oh, how I wanted to ascend those steps and sit, just once, to watch the movie from the balcony. One time, when Mr. Ruhlander was sweeping the steps during the second show, I found the gate open, but he stopped me before I could slip past him up the steps.

What I did not know, nor did anyone explain to me, was that only black people were allowed to sit in the balcony area. The box office, a glassed-in compartment under the left side of the marquee, had two slots in its window where tickets could be purchased: one for whites near the lobby door and the other for blacks on the opposite side near a small paneled door barely noticeable in the wall behind the movie poster displays. Inside this door, a set of bare, concrete steps dimly lit by naked lightbulbs rose up three flights, passing an unfinished single commode bathroom at the second level, with the top flight ending in the balcony. Three rows totaling about 20 seats at the rear left side of the balcony were separated from the front seats by a short wall and gate. This was the section for blacks.

I never saw a black person enter the theater. I was unaware they were even there. Their designated seating area could not be seen from the floor below. Because the bathroom on the second landing of the stairs was unfinished and blacks were not allowed to use the white restroom, they relieved themselves as necessary in the alley behind the theater. If they were allowed to buy popcorn, candy or soda, it was not from the concession stand in the lobby. I would like to think that Mr. Ruhlander delivered these refreshments to them. More than likely, he did not.

On the edge of my perfect fantasy world filled with pale, blonde movie stars and dreamy, handsome men was a dark reality hidden in the shadows of a forbidden place where I could not go.

Rest a Spell

1. How integrated was your life when you grew up? Did you have close friends of a different race or ethnic background?
2. What is prejudice? What causes us to be prejudiced? Is it possible to be totally free of prejudice?
3. How were the different races and ethnic groups (i.e., Latinos, African-Americans, American Indians, Italians) depicted in movies during the 1940s and 1950s? Have movies changed these stereotypes? If so, how?
4. The Disney Company has been under pressure to rerelease on DVD its classic film *Song of the South*, which features the adventures of Br'er Fox as narrated by Uncle Remus in Pidgin English. Should the movie be rereleased? Why, or why not?
5. Why do so many churches still remain segregated?

Walking With the Master

The young man, obviously in his early 20s, boarded the plane with his girlfriend in tow. As he slung his backpack around, he accidentally struck the lady across the aisle. Giving her a cursory glance, he mumbled a quick " 'scuse me." Then he fell into his seat, stretched out his long legs, crossed his sandal-clad feet out in the aisle, and began noisily consuming large quantities of food from his fast-food sack, supplemented by grapes from his girlfriend's stash. As they stole a clandestine kiss, I commented to my husband, "She's chasing her ducks to bad water – he's nothing but an immature, unmannerly lout who needs to grow up." Imagine my surprise when he pulled out his Bible and read it during the entire two-hour flight, underlining key passages.

A dictionary definition of prejudice identifies my attitude as "adverse judgment or opinion formed beforehand or without knowledge or examination of the facts" ("Prejudice"). Prejudice is often based on merely superficial characteristics. Our shallow judgment forms a stereotype that we have built on faulty inductive reasoning. In the past, we may have observed or been told about a few people who display a certain trait, and we infer that everyone who looks or acts similarly is the same. Our stereotypical thinking goes something like this: All gangly, unmannerly young men are too immature to make good mates. Therefore, this gangly, unmannerly young man will not make a good mate.

Whether the young man in question will make a good mate is based on his character and his compatibility with the young lady, and I, not knowing him personally, have no knowledge of that character or relationship. However, his seeming sincerity in studying God's Word certainly changed my perspective. Isn't it amazing how one action by another human being whom we do not know can change our opinion of that person? How prone we are to snap judgments. Prejudicial assessment of the character of others is what Jesus addresses in Matthew 7:1-2: "Judge not, that you be not judged. For with what judgment you judge, you will be judged; and with the measure you use, it will be measured back to you." He goes on to suggest that our intolerant attitudes and hypocrisy, as well as our other faults, may be much more serious sins in God's eyes than what we perceive as failings in others (vv. 3-5).

All of us are prejudiced to a greater or lesser degree. Our experiences in life – actual and virtual from both reading and viewing – form our emotional response to people and things. Although our intellect may tell us that our reasoning is flawed, our emotional response is so deeply embedded in our psyches that our biases are difficult to suppress. For example, most of us are extremely prejudiced against snakes – all varieties. Although we know that some snakes eat pesky insects and vermin and are actually beneficial, we still react out of fear when we see one. We have proclaimed all long, slithery, scaled reptiles to be of the same ilk as the venomous viper with poisonous fangs, and we run. We don't stick around long enough to become personally acquainted with the snake in question. Unfortunately, we react similarly to people who look, act or dress differently than we. We stereotype them as being undesirable and maybe even dangerous, and we run. We don't stick around long enough to become personally acquainted to see if we can find common ground as a basis for addressing our differences.

The younger we are when we form our prejudices, the more ingrained they are, and the harder we must work to overcome them. Our parents influence our prejudices from the time we are born. Although we may not actually hate people who are different, we are suspicious and wary of them. We sometimes forget that the generations who lived before and during the early 20th century were confined to a narrowly defined community with limited outside communication. Today our much broader, worldwide community exposes us to a variety of cultural backgrounds through our work, our schools and the media. The familial biases that were passed on to us are incompatible with our modern lifestyle where our very existence on this planet may depend on successful cooperation and conciliation as we negotiate with nations and ethnic groups who differ from us.

Truly, we must guard against the traditional prejudices of our families, communities and culture. We must both believe and act according to Paul's words: "There is neither Jew nor Greek, there is neither slave nor free, there is neither male nor female; for you are all one in Christ Jesus" (Galatians 3:28). In this verse, Paul identifies three categories of prejudice: xenophobia and/or racism, class bias and sexism.

• **Xenophobia.** The first of these is "xenophobia," an "unreasonable fear, distrust, or hatred of strangers, foreigners, or anything perceived as foreign or different" ("Xenophobe"). The key to this definition is the word "unreasonable." Obviously, during World War II we had reason to fear and distrust Hitler's Third Reich as well as the Japanese who attacked Pearl Harbor. Today, we have reason to fear and distrust the terrorists who attacked the World Trade Center in New York City. Patriotism, national pride and armed defense of our country are not xenophobic. Our attitude toward Muslim nations today is perhaps justified and not xenophobic because theirs is a war against Christianity.

In the Old Testament, God commanded His people to remain separate from the nations around them because they would be tempted to worship idols and false gods. Although it may be best to keep ourselves separate, at the same time we must be careful not to hate our enemies (Matthew 5:44). Furthermore, when time changes circumstance, we must not continue to act prejudicially toward those nationalities that fought against us in the past. Forgiveness is extremely difficult when we have been touched personally by tragic loss, but forgiveness, like love, is commanded (6:14-15). How can we not forgive our enemies when Christ prayed on the cross: "Father, forgive them, for they do not know what they do" (Luke 23:34)?

With the advent of illegal immigration in the United States, Mexicans have now become the new target of xenophobes. Despite our political leanings, lest we carry our patriotism too far, we must remember that even the law of Moses did not support the mistreatment of foreigners: "Also you shall not oppress a stranger, for you know the heart of a stranger, because you were strangers in the land of Egypt" (Exodus 23:9). God, through Jeremiah, reiterated this attitude: "Execute judgment and righteousness, and deliver the plundered out of the hand of the oppressor. Do no wrong and do no violence to the stranger, the fatherless, or the widow, nor shed innocent blood in this place" (Jeremiah 22:3).

Providing for strangers was also encouraged when landowners were told, "When you reap the harvest of your land, you shall not wholly reap the corners of your field ... nor shall you gather any gleaning. ... You shall leave them for the poor and for the stranger" (Leviticus 23:22). Ruth, a native of Moab, gleaned the grain that was left in the fields of Boaz in accordance with this law (Ruth 2).

Just as in our society today, Nehemiah faced the problem of foreign languages when the Jews married women of Ashdod, Ammon and Moab: "And half of their children spoke the language of Ashdod, and could not speak the language of Judah, but spoke according to the language of one or the other people" (Nehemiah 13:23-24). Perhaps to avoid the confusion that resulted from different languages in Nehemiah's day and at the tower of Babel (Genesis 11:6-9), all Americans would be better served by learning to speak one language. However, our job as Christians is the Great Commission (Matthew 28:19-20), no matter the language or nationality. Those churches that provide worship and teaching for non-English-speaking sojourners in our land, whether they are here legally or illegally, are to be commended for placing their Christian duty first before all other considerations.

• **Racism.** Closely akin to xenophobia is "racism," "a belief or doctrine that inherent differences among the various human so-called races determine cultural or individual achievement, usually involving the idea that one's own race is superior" ("Racism"). Whether or not we want to admit it, racism is rampant in our nation, most especially toward African-Americans. Such attitudes are most often associated with the South, but racism rears its ugly head in northern states as well.

Although racism is no longer as overt as it was in the 1950s when blacks were confined to a theater balcony, more subtle racist practices do still occur. One such practice is racial steering, in which a real estate agent shows homes in white neighborhoods to whites, Latino neighborhoods to Latinos, and black neighborhoods to African-Americans. Because fair-housing laws prohibit giving out information about race and demographics in a neighborhood, the property purchaser can be steered to what is considered by the realtor as more compatible neighborhoods (Baker).

Racial epithets still abound as well, as was evident in April 2007 when Don Imus, a radio personality, made inappropriate remarks about the Rutgers women's basketball team. One unintentional benefit from this incident was that the academic achievements and good character of the young women were spotlighted, making Imus' bigotry look boorish and absurd in contrast.

Strangely in both the North and the South, the Lord's church remains segregated into mostly black and mostly white congregations. One hopes this separation is because of preferred worship style and not because of prejudice. Unfortunately, it may also be a result of the segregated communities in which we often live. All of us, I am sure, welcome visitors from other racial and ethnic backgrounds to worship with us. My husband and I have never been more royally treated than we were several years ago at a black congregation in Rochester, N.Y. The friendliness of the ladies who went the extra mile in making us feel welcomed remains one of our dearest memories. Surely, if our Christian hospitality is so warmly offered to visitors, it extends as well to members within our local congregations.

• **Class Bias.** Class bias is also mentioned by Paul in Galatians 3:28. Today, our biases depend upon our own socio-economic status. The rich see the poor as cheap labor; the poor see the rich as greedy. Meanwhile, those in the middle see the rich as owning the politicians who enact laws to benefit the wealthy and the poor as taking undue advantage of social programs not available to the middle class. To paraphrase Nathanael in John 1:46, they ask, "Can anything good come out of Washington?" The answer to this question, of course, is colored by our income, our political views and our personal belief system. Proverbs points out that "The rich and the poor have this in common, The Lord is the maker of them all" (22:2), and James tells us to treat all men with the same respect:

> My brethren, do not hold the faith of our Lord Jesus Christ, the Lord of glory, with partiality. For if there should come into your assembly a man with gold rings, in fine apparel, and there should also come in a poor man in filthy clothes, and you pay attention to the one wearing the fine clothes and say to him, "You sit here in a good place," and say to the poor man, "You stand there," or, "Sit here at my footstool," have you not shown partiality among yourselves, and become judges with evil thoughts? (2:1-4)

He continues by pointing out that the poor are often richer in faith and that showing partiality is a sin (James 2:5, 9). Today, perhaps more than ever, we must guard against judging someone according to superficial social strata rather than simple, unadorned spirituality. The emphasis in our society on owning an abundance of things makes us vulnerable to making a distinction between the "haves" and the "have nots."

• **Sexism.** The equality of men and women in Christ mentioned in Galatians 3:28 certainly opposes the type of prejudice known as sexism. In this age of women's rights, the definition has been narrowly defined as "prejudice against the female sex." However, a broader second definition is more applicable: "arbitrary stereotyping of males and females on the basis of their gender" ("Sexism"). After all, women can be as prejudicial toward men as men toward women. I recognize, for example, my own sexist attitude toward male gynecologists because I doubt their ability to understand my concerns as a woman. Despite my gender preference for a female gynecologist, however, I respect the many male physicians who have treated me over the years.

It is important that we accept that gender has little to do with success in most professions. At the same time, we must remember that God created us male and female to be uniquely suited for complementary roles both in the home and in the church. These roles do not mean that either sex is less intelligent or less talented or that in many activities one sex is more capable than the other. We each have an important niche to fill. Nor does God condone one gender demeaning or mistreating the other through hurtful words or actions.

No matter the type of prejudice, and there are too many to mention, it is sinful in God's eyes. We must remember that God is the Maker of us all: "For who makes you differ from another? And what do you have that you did not receive?" (1 Corinthians 4:7). If God saw fit to make us different, then who are we to question that difference or to place higher value on one of His creations over another? When addressing the variety of gifts given to members of the early church, Paul admonishes each of them "not to think of himself more highly than he ought to think" (Romans 12:3-8). We are to make the most of every opportunity to "do good to all, especially to those who are of the household of faith" (Galatians 6:10). After all, God is not prejudiced. As Peter told Cornelius and his household, "God shows no partiality. But in every nation whoever fears Him and works righteousness is accepted by Him" (Acts 10:34-35).

Shod With the Preparation of the Gospel

1. Discuss stereotypes of mothers-in-law, Southerners, lawyers, and Christians. Name other stereotypes and their supposed characteristics.
2. Read the following passages and discuss snap judgments or prejudices displayed in each.
   • John 1:45-46
   • 1 Samuel 1:12-16
   • Numbers 12:1-2
   • Ecclesiastes 7:27-28
   • Matthew 15:21-28
3. Discuss the meaning of each of the following scriptures and how it can be applied to prejudice.
   • Proverbs 18:1-2
   • Proverbs 28:21
   • Ephesians 4:11-13
   • 1 John 2:9-11
   • Romans 14:1-13
4. Today in our churches, do we give more attention to visitors or prospective members who are prosperous or prominent in society?

99 • PROCESSING PREJUDICE

5. As an author, my greatest worry in writing this chapter was whether
   I was being offensive in my terminology. How important is "political correctness" to communication? Can we discuss our differences
   without being worried about offending or without taking offense?

Chapter 10

Working
As for the LORD

*"Whatever you do, work at it with all your heart,
as working for the Lord, not for men."*
(Colossians 3:23 NIV)

Barefoot With Dolly

My mother, being from some ancient school of womanhood, had very rigid ideas about what a young lady should or should not do. This included not only dress and manners but types of work as well. My options were limited in my younger years.

The clothes were bad enough. I was never allowed to wear pants to school because ladies were expected to wear dresses. It mattered not that I would be flipping upside down on the jungle gym – had she seen me, she would have thought that was not ladylike either. And she said absolutely no Barbie doll. Mother thought she was disgraceful with her Betty Grable, pin-up-girl shape. When I matured earlier than normal in my preteen years, my mother was both surprised and horrified. Her little girl was growing up too fast. Consequently, I was nearly 16 before I was allowed to wear a more figure-revealing, straight skirt in lieu of a gathered one with cancan petticoats.

Mother also had definite ideas about the type of work appropriate for young ladies. She considered housework to be woman's work whereas mowing and gardening were for men only. Yes, she was proud of the beautiful flowers and shrubs that graced our yard, but she actually only planned it all. My dad and brother were merely peons who dug the holes where they were told. Indoors was her domain, and she made it mine as well.

Each Saturday I was given a choice of chores: I could either dust or vacuum; she would do the opposite. I usually picked vacuuming. It was certainly easier than crawling around ornately carved chair and table legs with a bottle of O-Cedar furniture polish and a dust rag made from one of my dad's undershirts. We had a canister Electrolux with sleigh runners that was pulled by a long gray vacuum hose with its various attachments. The hard part was getting the canister around chairs and door facings without scarring them. Our rugs were surrounded on all sides by a hardwood floor border, which meant using a different attachment for each. Luckily, the light pine wood and the gray leaf design of the rugs didn't show the dirt I missed.

The washing machines in the basement were even more difficult to operate. We had two of these contraptions, an older model that had lost its wringer but still swished the clothes back and forth in its dull, gray metal tub, and a white enamel newer model trimmed in red. The older model was used for washing, the newer for rinsing. Then the clothes were fed through the rollers on the wringer to land in a damp pile in a No. 3 galvanized washtub on the other side. Feeding the wringer was a tricky business for little fingers, and my mother would not allow me to do it until I was a teenager. The clothes were then carried in the tubs to be hung on the clothesline. In my preschool years, I enjoyed running between the sheets hanging on the lines that ran four deep across our backyard.

By the time I turned 10, I was assigned the ironing for the family. Although I was a little young to be handling a iron, I was taught not to touch the hot metal, just as I had been taught at an earlier age not to stick my hand in the blades of the open-guard, electric fan. Since we did not have a steam iron, we caught water in our fingers from the kitchen faucet or used a sprinkler lid on a bottle to dampen the clothes for ironing. Then we wrapped them in a recycled dry-cleaner bag and placed them in the refrigerator to prevent mold from growing until they could be ironed. I first learned to iron pillowcases, napkins and my dad's handkerchiefs. From there, I graduated to the sheets and table-cloths. Much later, I could press Dad's shirts.

Knowing how to sew was important too. My first attempt at a cross-stitched duck on a dish towel won a red ribbon at the county fair when I was 9. An apron was my first project using our old sewing machine. Because starting the movement of the needle and bobbin with the foot-operated treadle took coordination that did not come easily, my dad bought a new electric machine. I improved my skills through 4-H projects like skirts, blouses, vests and finally dresses. Many of these projects were made from chicken-feed sacks that came in various printed designs on cotton. One of my more embarrassing moments occurred at the state fair when I fainted while standing in a long line waiting to model my dress for the judges.

Etiquette was also important at our house. I was taught at an early age how to use the telephone properly. To reach the local exchange, we would rotate the ringer on the side of the telephone quickly, then wait politely for Mr. or Mrs. Nix to ask, "Number, please?" Our home phone number was 21, my dad's store was 26, and my Aunt Billie's number was 37. However, these numbers were not pronounced "twenty-one," or "twenty-six" or "thirty-seven." For clarity, I suppose, we were to say "two-six, please" or "three-seven, please." The word "please" was part of the number in our household. Many times we would have to ring again because a line would be shared by several parties, and it would be busy. Although I rarely called from a party line, Mother taught me it was impolite to listen in on other's conversations. As a teenager when I phoned my friends in nearby Lawrenceburg on one of the two lines available, Mr. Nix would interrupt with, "Dolly, I need the line, please," and I would immediately close the conversation to let someone else use the line.

Table etiquette and a properly set table were also important in our home. We never sat down to eat at a bare table, even for breakfast in the kitchen. Our table was covered by cotton or linen tablecloths, not the more commonly used oilcloth. Each place was properly set with a knife, a fork and a spoon whether needed or not. We had an older set of silver-plate utensils for everyday use and a nicer set for dining room occasions. Eating at the dining table on Sundays, which usually included a preacher or other visitors, demanded the use of Granny's cro-cheted tablecloth, our nicer dishes and stemmed crystal. In the kitchen we used dishes that came free with groceries and drank from peanut butter glasses decorated with cartoon characters or flower designs.

Recycling, before recycling became politically correct, was a way of life that did not preclude propriety even in a middle-class, modest home. The key to practicing the social graces with economy was con-tinuous and repetitive work – washing, polishing, dusting, vacuuming, mopping, cleaning and sewing. However, the work was not so impor-tant that it could not be interrupted in an instant. Mother would often have both washing machines going when Dad would appear at the base-ment door with "Let's go fishing." Mother would unplug both machines, and in 15 minutes we would be on our way to Pickwick Dam on the Tennessee River. The rest of the day would be spent with my mother and dad standing on their favorite rocks with rod and reel in hand while I played on shore. Woman's work could wait for another day.

Rest a Spell

1. Our work in the home has obviously been made easier by modern conveniences. What appliances do you appreciate most? Why?
2. How has the woman's role in housework changed over the years? What about the man's role?
3. How has table etiquette changed? What developments in our socie-ty have changed table etiquette? Is etiquette still important?
4. Discuss telephone etiquette. What new rules would we apply to cell phone use?
5. How much responsibility should children have toward the upkeep of their homes? What skills do we need to be passing on to them?
6. What are some items that you recycle by putting to use in a new way? Do you participate in organized recycling? Is recycling important?
7. How can we make sure our children grow up with good work habits?
8. Dolly lived and worked in what would be considered an unsafe en-vironment (i.e. open-grill electric fans). Does the emphasis on safe-ty today impede a child's understanding of danger?

Walking With the Master

Deadlines aren't what they used to be. The very word deadline implies, "Step over this line, and you are dead." However, in the modern vernacular, a deadline is something that can be moved and then, if still inconvenient, moved again. Thus, procrastination is rewarded. Not so for my son Brian. As a 5-year-old, he was assigned the task of storing his toys on the shelves in his room. Periodically, I would check on his progress and find him in the floor playing with them rather than putting them away. His procrastination continued until one day while he was gone from home, the Spic and Span Fairy came to our house and carried away everything left on the floor. Consequently, the mere mention of her reappearance, even in jest, would get him on task even as a teenager.

We all need motivation to complete the task at hand, whether pleasant or unpleasant. God understands man's need for employment. He immediately gave Adam work with a purpose: "Then the Lord God took the man and put him in the garden of Eden to tend and keep it" (Genesis 2:15). Surprisingly, work, a four-letter word for many people, is necessary to man's happiness. The poet Marge Piercy, in her poem "To Be of Use," expresses that need: "The pitcher cries for water to carry / and a person for work that is real."

All labor is real if it embodies a spiritual purpose. God's Word provides us with motivation for purposeful work, even in our secular vocations. Two key verses appear in Colossians 3. First of all, we are told in verse 17 that "whatever you do in word or deed, do all in the name of the Lord Jesus." A few verses later, Paul adds, "And whatever you do, do it heartily, as to the Lord and not to men" (v. 23). If we could approach everything we do with the idea that we are working for God, not for ourselves or for men, our priorities would be in order and our product would be our best effort. Although our choice of employment would perhaps remain the same, it would be imbued with a higher purpose: to be a true servant of God as we work with and serve others.

A favorite saying in our family is "if it's worth doing, it's worth doing right." That principle was and is applied to all activities, whether making a bed, folding clothes, mowing the lawn, doing homework, preparing to teach a lesson, or attending worship. Planning ahead is the key to success in all work – plan the work; work the plan. The wise writer of Proverbs says, "The plans of the diligent lead surely to plenty, But those of everyone who is hasty, surely to poverty" (21:5). Haste, in all activities, truly ends up being waste, and haste is often the product of a lack of purpose and the resulting procrastination. We must recognize a hierarchy of purpose in our lives and prioritize our activities accordingly. If I must make a choice between making up a bed and getting to Sunday morning worship on time, the bed will be left unmade. If I think both are important, by planning ahead I will simply rise earlier and be able to accomplish both. However, worship takes precedence. Tardiness is a form of procrastination and demonstrates a lack of purpose. Prioritizing based on purpose will lead us to the preparation necessary to solve this problem.

We can study the first chapters of Nehemiah and learn a lesson in planning a work and then working according to that plan.

• **Determine the Purpose.** First of all, Nehemiah saw a purpose – a need. When he asked Hanani and other Judeans who came to Persia about the conditions back home, he learned that the wall of Jerusalem was "broken down and the gates … burned with fire" (Nehemiah 1:3). He was so distressed that he cried. Then he prayed. Anything we do involves prayer to keep us in touch with the will of our heavenly Father. He will guide our daily lives and help us prioritize our activities according to His purpose, not ours. E. Stanley Jones says that prayer "is surrender – surrender to the will of God and cooperation with that will. If I throw out a boat hook from a boat and catch hold of the shore and pull, do I pull the shore to me? Or, do I pull myself to shore? Prayer is not pulling God to my will, but the aligning of my will to the will of God" ("Prayer" 453).

With God's help through a vigilant prayer life, we can eliminate some of the busyness in our lives through prioritizing. Abraham Lincoln, in a discussion of tariffs, observed:

> The habits of our whole species fall into three great classes – useful labour, useless labour, and idleness. Of these the first only is meritorious; and to it all the products of labor rightfully belong; but the two latter, while they exist, are heavy pensioners upon the first, robbing it of a large portion

of its just rights. The only remedy for this is to, as far as possible, drive useless labour and idleness out of existence. (*Collected*, 1:412)

When we "do all in the name of the Lord Jesus," the useless labor and idleness will disappear from our agenda, and all the jobs remaining will be truly useful.

• **Set a Deadline.** When Nehemiah explained to the king of Persia his purpose for returning to Judea and asked permission to rebuild the walls of Jerusalem, the king inquired how long he would be gone. Nehemiah "set him a time" or gave him a specific time frame for the project (2:6). Without a deadline, the work might never have been completed. C. Northcote Parkinson, a British economist, is known for Parkinson's Law: "Work expands so as to fill the time available for its completion." In other words, the more time we have, the less we get done at any given moment. This principle perhaps explains why busy people accomplish more than those who have more time available to accomplish a task, but don't. Today, deadlines, if we take them seriously, frame our assignments and keep them from expanding until they consume all our time and other's time as well. Self-motivation is fine for those who have been blessed with a healthy helping of it, but most of us need motivation from outside forces, at least for those jobs we deem an onus. We do ourselves and our children a disservice when we allow ourselves and them to ignore the time frame for completing an assignment, whether it be for home, for school or especially for church. We should first be a good example for our children and then function as the enforcer of deadlines for them. Although it is often difficult, we need to step aside and let our children pay the consequences for missing a deadline at school without intervening for them with excuses.

Excuses are enablers. "The dog ate my homework" becomes "something came up," or "I didn't really understand," or "I don't have enough ability to do that," or "I wasn't in a good mood." The writer of Proverbs makes fun of the absurdity of our excuses in 22:13: "The lazy man says, 'There is a lion outside! I shall be slain in the streets!' " No matter what excuse we give, what we really mean is "I just didn't want to do it."

• **Cogitate Before Commencing.** Nehemiah accessed the situation before beginning the work. He went at night with a few companions, telling no one about his mission, to survey the damaged walls for himself (2:12-16). All of us need some "mulling time" when facing a task – time to access, to muse, to cogitate, to think through the process. Too many a hasty worker has "painted himself into a corner" with no way out. We must think before we speak and before we act. Some quiet time spent alone with our thoughts will bring out the best that we and God have to offer. There is much truth in the saying "Sleep on it." Many a time, I have gone to bed with a project on my mind, only to wake in the early morning hours with an unforeseen solution. Somewhere deep in our psyches are resources that, with God's help, we can delve into subconsciously if we will only be quiet and listen. However, if we are merely procrastinating, putting off until tomorrow the commencement of our work, the time is wasted.

• **Motivate Co-Workers.** Nehemiah communicated the problem to the people, motivating them with his well-chosen words (2:17-18). The best motivations in any work are a need and being needed. When co-workers see a need, they will have "a mind to work" (4:6). However, they must also feel needed as well. Sometimes we wonder why we must do all the work ourselves when we simply have not asked others to share in it. Nehemiah divided the task among the workers. Similarly, in the Corinthian church, Paul admonished each Christian to find his niche in the body of Christ and to work without concern for recognition or pre-eminence (1 Corinthians 12:12-27). Even today, we should examine our role in the most important organization on earth, the church: Which part am I? What is my specific purpose within the body? Do I have "a mind to work"? Or am I handicapping the work by not functioning in my role or by demanding more attention than is necessary? A willing spirit and teamwork are essentials in both secular and spiritual work.

• **Organize the Work.** William Shakespeare, in his historical play *Henry V*, says, "So work the honey-bees, / Creatures that by a rule in nature teach / The act of order to a peopled kingdom" (1.2.187-89). God's creation and its creatures understand and respect the orderly rule of nature, and so should we. After assigning various sections of the wall to different workers, indicated by the words "next to them" in the first portion of chapter 3, Nehemiah repeats the words "after him" several times in the last half of the chapter to designate the chronology of the building tasks. Sometimes we want to skip what we consider the hard, unrewarding part of our work and jump to the end without the necessary steps leading to success. Students in school often do this. They want to skip the homework that lays the foundation and practice for true understanding and just memorize the facts for the test. Therefore, when the test requires the application of skills to a new problem, the student fails. Similarly, when asked to write a composition, many students will hand in their first effort without going through the processes of revision and editing. Unfortunately, the tendency to skip steps and finish as quickly as possible has carried over into the marketplace, where product recalls have cost industries billions of dollars.

• **Defend Work Against Detractors.** Sometimes, like Nehemiah, our work must be guarded. The world is full of naysayers who will find fault with our plans, interfere with our work, and point out all the possible pitfalls in completing a project. First, Sanballat and Tobiah scoffed at the idea of building a wall and laughed and ridiculed the workers (2:19). Then they said the work was inferior and the wall would be too weak to even deter a fox (4:3). Finally, they stirred up a mob from among the enemy nations to attack the builders and cause confusion (4:7-8). As a result, Nehemiah put guards on the walls for protection, and every worker stayed prepared with a sword for defense at hand. In addition to the opposition of Sanballat and Tobiah, Nehemiah also had to contend with governmental corruption and usury, burdening the poor citizens with excessive taxes (5:1-13).

Even after Nehemiah became governor, he had to contend with falsehoods from the rumor-mills of his day whom he told, "No such things as you say are being done, but you invent them in your own heart" (6:8). Similarly, we face the adversaries in our workplaces today who criticize our sincere efforts and then, if the criticism does not have the desired effect, spread rumors and falsehoods. The news media are a prime example of those who criticize and distort the truth for the sole purpose of advancing themselves. There are also those who will belittle us and make us question the work we do, but like Nehemiah, we must continue when we know what we do is our best effort given for the right purpose.

As individuals employed in the secular workplace, each one of us must be the best employee she knows how to be as a member of the team. It is on the job that we probably can influence more people for the Lord. Our attitudes, our words, our demeanor and especially our work ethic will be a measure of our Christianity. Nothing is more irritating to fellow workers than a sluggard who does not carry out her duties in an efficient and timely fashion.

The Bible addresses slothfulness both in the Old and New Testaments. Proverbs says that a lazy man is like "vinegar to the teeth and smoke to the eyes" (10:26). Although the sluggard likes lying in bed, he does not sleep well because of inactivity: "As a door turns on its hinges, So does the lazy man on his bed" (26:14). The home (and office cubicle) of a lazy man is easily recognizable: it is "all overgrown with thorns; Its surface [is] covered with nettles; Its stone wall [is] broken down" (24:31). Because of his laziness, "the building decays, And through idleness of hands the house leaks" (Ecclesiastes 10:18). Perhaps the most telling description of a lazy man is in his physical stance – he "buries his hand in the bowl [armpit]" – and in his opinion he is wiser "than seven men who can answer sensibly" (Proverbs 26:15-16). Idleness, as expressed in an adage, is the devil's playground. It leads the young, who are by nature active, into trouble with the authorities, and it produces in adults a tendency to gossip and waste time. Workers who take too many breaks at the water cooler can become like the Athenians who "spent their time in nothing else but either to tell or to hear some new thing" (Acts 17:21).

We are expected to work and do the best with what we have. Paul instructs the early church: "If anyone will not work, neither shall he eat" (2 Thessalonians 3:10), and he tells Timothy that "if anyone does not provide for his own, and especially for those of his household, he has denied the faith and is worse than an unbeliever" (1 Timothy 5:8). We can rest from our labors, for rest is good: in the beginning God designated one day of rest for Himself from the work of creating (Genesis 2:2). If He needed time off from His work, so do we. However, when we are rejuvenated, we must work with all our might as "for the Lord, not for men" (Colossians 3:23 NIV).

Shod With the Preparation of the Gospel

1. What are some of the complaints people have about the necessity of work? Are these valid complaints? How can they improve their attitude and productivity?
2. Share a time when you worked with a group and someone let the group down by not doing an assigned part. How did you feel toward that person? How did you compensate for the lack of participation?
3. What is the difference in an excuse and a reason? Establish criteria for determining the difference.
4. How does preparation help us in every aspect of life?
   • Do you prepare for a vacation? For work? For Bible study as a student? For worship?
   • Have you prepared for sudden illness or accident? For death? For the second coming of the Lord?
5. Read carefully all the work accomplished by the woman in Proverbs 31. What do you think is the total span of time covered in this description? Compare the passage with Ecclesiastes 3:1-8.
6. As an individual or as a group, use the steps given from the book of Nehemiah to plan a project within the context of the Lord's work (i.e., a fellowship, a ladies visitation program, a ladies mission trip).

Chapter 11

Nature's NURTURE

*"But now ask the beasts, and they will teach you;
And the birds of the air, and they will tell you."
(Job 12:7)*

Barefoot With Dolly

When I needed solitude or just wanted to get away from my mother in my preteen years, the chicken house was my refuge. Balanced in a wheelbarrow as if it were my high-back throne, I would sit with the handles and back legs on the ground, lean back against the bottom with the sides cupping my shoulders, and soak up the warm sunshine. I was further comforted by the gentle, sympathetic clucking of the hens around me.

We had three chicken houses. The oldest was a small block structure with a high floor and half door to protect the hens from night raiders. Under this floor a mother skunk once decided to raise her young. Daddy put a garden hose in the tailpipe of his car, ran it under the floor, and asphyxiated the family. He pulled up the floorboards, and my brother and I had our photograph made holding the dead skunks by their tails – a big mistake since our clothes had to be buried to remove the stench.

The next chicken house to be built had three rooms: one for laying hens, one for pullets, and an upstairs room for baby chicks. We waited with impatient anticipation for the boxes of babies to arrive by railway car. Each box was filled with a carpet of yellow fur balls that were more than happy to be released onto the litter-covered floor. There they would run in golden waves, 200 at a time, around the warm brooder, pausing briefly to drink water from dishes fed by upside down glass gallon jugs. Gathering in clusters, they would nap before breaking ranks for another run. Only when they were pullets and old enough to descend the steps to the lower floor without hurting themselves would we release them for the next phase of life.

Our third chicken house was open air with walls made of poultry wire that honeycombed the breezes blowing from the clover field where the hens could graze in summer. Long green tarpaulins tied up in huge rolls with twine could be released to keep the icy winter winds out. It was my job to gather the eggs from the aluminum nesting boxes lining the inner walls. Periodically, a proud hen would emerge from a straw-lined nest, strut her stuff, and boast loudly about her egg-laying talent. I preferred the braggarts to the silent, sullen hens that refused to move off the nest but instead pecked at my hand as I stole the eggs. I became quite adept at grabbing for the offending bill with one hand and the eggs with the other.

Despite the acrid smell of chicken litter on the concrete floor and the dust-dipped cobwebs suspended from the redwood rafters overhead, I found this chicken house to be a cheerful place. Every time I arrived with empty egg buckets, I was greeted with such loud singing that a human conversation could not have been heard. As I waded through a sea of Rhode Island Reds or New Hampshires to dip buckets of feed from the storage drums into their troughs and to open the spigots for fresh water, every throat would be opened in a joyful noise. The hens would cluster around my feet to brush their feathers against me, making it difficult to walk. I was their queen; they made me feel special.

Many of the hens became my special pets. Old Blindy, who had one white fish eye, was a particular favorite, along with Wattles, Crossbeak, and Miss Sassy. We valued our good layers. My brother even saved one with an emergency operation. She had developed a growth in her craw. Granny held her on her back on an upside down washtub while Corky opened her with a single-edge razor blade. He removed the growth and sewed her up with one of my mother's needles and strong black thread.

She went back immediately to the other hens in the chicken yard and lived to lay more eggs.

When it came time to sell the older laying hens, I could not bear to be near the chicken houses as the men grabbed them up in twos and threes, sometimes breaking a wing or a leg, to throw them on a truck for market. The fear in their loud cries broke my heart. I also went to the front yard when the pullets were killed for Sunday dinner or for my mother to can in jars. String nooses hung permanently from the clothesline in the backyard where the latest to be slaughtered were suspended upside down by their feet. Then my dad would cut off their heads with a butcher knife and let them bleed out. Sometimes one would escape the noose and flop around in the backyard, trying to walk without a head. It was a gruesome sight.

The only slaughter I did not mind, and actually applauded, was the permanent removal of whatever rooster ruled the chicken yard at the time. I don't know why we kept a rooster unless it was simply to torment me. When they lived in the yard, I was presented with two hazards simultaneously to be avoided: the brown and white swirls of hen droppings littering the ground and an imminent rooster attack. Prissy Pants and Big Red were the worst offenders. I would approach the gate only when they were at the most distant point in the yard and then make a dash for the chicken house. No matter where these two were, they would come running after me with glistening spurs and flapping wings. I was petrified. My brother was better at defending himself. One time he picked Prissy Pants up by the tail, carried him to the fence, and dropped him on the other side. I wasn't brave enough to get that close.

Despite the occasional presence of a mean rooster, the chicken houses were a haven from the pressures of growing up. The money wasn't bad either. My 4-H poultry project was the best in the state, and the proceeds from egg sales paid my way through college. I was even interviewed for a national radio broadcast on CBS – in the chicken house with all my hens joyfully singing their support in the background.

Rest a Spell

1. If you grew up in a rural area, share your experiences with farm animals.

2. What types of pets have you and your family owned throughout the years? Did you own them, or did they "own" you?

3. Why do some people prefer cats and others prefer dogs? You might find it interesting to research White House pets and how preferences have changed in the history of the presidency.

4. How has care for both pets and farm animals changed during your lifetime?

5. Are Americans more concerned about their personal pets than they are about human beings?

6. What are some lessons you have learned by observing or interacting with animals?

Walking With the Master

I like to think that our cat Tiger loves us. He rubs our toes and curls around our legs to give us what seems like a feline hug. However, I have my doubts. After all, he rubs the cabinet base, the refrigerator door, his food container and his bowl with the same fervor he applies to us. I have a strong suspicion that I am merely another territory he marks with his scent.

We all like to ascribe human emotions to our favorite pets and forget that their actions are basically instinctive. We can train them through repetitive reward or discomfort to behave and perform in ways that please us – we hope. Tiger was hugged tightly as a kitten and imprisoned in a blanket by an 8-year-old "mother" as a substitute baby doll. As a result, he avoids being held or hugged as an adult cat. With patience, we strive to retrain him by holding him for brief moments and then letting him go at his will, not ours. Freedom of choice is basic to a feline's nature – just ask any cat owner.

God has given us animals for multiple reasons: to provide us with food, to serve us by aiding our work, to comfort us with companionship, and to teach us. He, therefore, expects us to treat all animals with the respect that is due His creations. While we stand in awe of the natural forces of our environment that "declare the glory of God" and show "His handiwork" (Psalm 19:1), His created beings who breathe the same oxygen we breathe and have a life span that ends in death as ours do form a special relationship with us as we share this planet.

• **Animals Provide Food.** Animals, ultimately, are our responsibility. After creating all the animals on the sixth day, God shaped man from the dust of the earth and said, "Let Us make man in Our image, according to Our likeness; let them have dominion over the fish of the sea, over the birds of the air, and over the cattle, over all the earth and over every creeping thing that creeps on the earth" (Genesis 1:26). Before the flood, no fear of man or other beast is evident; animals and man probably coexisted harmoniously. Evidently all were vegetarian because Genesis 1:29-30 tells us God gave herbs and fruits as food to all the mammals and birds as well as to man. Only after the flood did God give the fear and dread of mankind to animals, birds and fish; also at that time He allowed man to eat meat: "Every moving thing that lives shall be food for you. I have given you all things, even as the green herbs. But you shall not eat flesh with its life, that is, its blood" (Genesis 9:3-4). More than likely, at this same time some animals were modified to be carnivorous.

Although some people would deny others the right to eat meat or use animal products, God ordained meat and animal products as food for mankind. Proverbs instructs the farmer to tend his flocks carefully because after the harvest when winter comes, the lambs and goats will provide milk, food and clothing for his entire household (27:23-27). Numerous examples abound in the Scriptures demonstrating that God's chosen people ate the meat of clean animals as directed by Him.

Hunting practices were also addressed. Although eggs could be taken from a nest, the mother bird was not to be taken or harmed (Deuteronomy 22:6-7). This principle is practiced today in managed hunts where females, so necessary to the survival of a species, are often protected. The wise writer of Proverbs also condemns wasting meat from a hunt: "The lazy man does not roast what he took in hunting" (12:27). Today, taking the head, horns or antlers of a trophy game animal and leaving the meat behind is illegal.

Meanwhile, the Old Law forbade man to mistreat or misuse animals. Even if an animal belonged to an enemy, the Israelites were instructed to behave in a humane way. A lost animal, when found, should be led back to its owner, or if the animal had fallen under its burden, it should be helped (Exodus 23:4-5). Beasts of burden were also to rest on the seventh day at the same time as their owners (v. 12). Proverbs 12:10 praises the righteous man who "regards the life of his animal" and condemns the cruelty of the wicked.

Several studies have been conducted to show that cruelty to animals has been linked to violent acts toward humans. One such study was conducted at the University of South Florida by Kathleen Heide, professor of criminology and a licensed mental health counselor, in conjunction with animal welfare expert Linda Merz-Perez. The study shows a direct correlation between animal cruelty and interpersonal violence. The 100 randomly chosen inmates at a maximum security facility reported such activities as "stomping a kitten to death, setting a dog on fire, and having sex with an animal." Thirty-three percent of the men in the study were convicted of murder, manslaughter or attempted murder while 31 percent were convicted of sexual battery. The rest were convicted of other violent offenses. Heide and Perez concluded that childhood intervention through exercises to develop empathy with animals could have perhaps changed the violent paths chosen by these convicts (Cobas).

• **Animals Provide Comfort and Companionship.** All children can benefit from the training that comes from caring for and interacting with a pet, thus learning the gentleness and kindness needed in loving and caring for other humans. Although some pets are perhaps chosen based on novelty and may be questionable choices for interaction (i.e., snakes, lizards, fish), even the most exotic of choices can at least teach responsibility. However, a well-chosen bird or docile mammal provides the added pleasure of touch, which enhances learning. Kindness and respect lead to favorable relationships, whereas rough treatment and harshness lead to unfavorable consequences – a growl, a nipped finger or withdrawal. Similar retaliation is communicated in human relations through words and unfriendly reactions.

Older people benefit from the companionship of animals as well. Many assisted-living residences and rest homes have found that stroking or playing with a cat or small dog adds pleasure to the lives of the elderly, even those with severe dementia. Comfort and companionship are the most frequently stated reasons for pet ownership, and obviously Americans truly feel a need for the contentment added by a pet. In 2003 the American Pet Products Manufacturers Association reported that 62 percent of households own a pet and 47 percent of those same households own more than one kind of animal. Dogs and cats, of course, are the leading types of pets, followed by a much smaller percentage of fish, birds, small animals and reptiles. The care of these animals cost Americans $31 billion in 2003, an estimated $460 per pet-owning household. The main expenditures of animal ownership are veterinarian care, food and supplies (Anderson 58).

Unfortunately, many Americans go overboard in pampering their pets, carrying the biblically commanded care to a sinful excess. Designer clothes for dogs and cats include faux fur, Burberry plaid knockoffs, Halloween and holiday costumes, as well as monogrammed feeding dishes and bedding. Owners take their furry pets to doggy spas where they have massages, drink herbal teas and get beauty treatments, and pets have been known to receive edible greeting cards. One-third of households owning small animals consider them as family members (Anderson 58). Sixty-three percent of owners say "I love you" to their pets every day, and 83 percent even refer to themselves as their pets' mom or dad (Anderson 60). Add to these the pet cemeteries with elaborate funerals and stone memorials and the recent interest in cloning a favorite pet, and we have modern animal worship reminiscent of that condemned in the Old Law: "Take careful heed to yourselves … lest you act corruptly and make for yourselves a carved image in the form of any figure: … the likeness of any animal that is on the earth or the likeness of any winged bird that flies in the air … And take heed lest you … feel driven to worship them and serve them" (Deuteronomy 4:15-19).

Although we cannot help mourning the loss of a beloved pet, we must remember that our favorite cat or dog is simply what it is – an animal – and despite the fact that some in our society today claim that pets have souls and will go to heaven, such a belief is erroneous. In fact, in Bible times among God's people, our favorite pets, the cat and dog, were shunned. The term "dog" was actually used as an insult: in the Old Testament it refers to a male prostitute (Deuteronomy 23:18); in the New Testament it is the term applied to Gentiles by Jews (Matthew 15:26); and in Revelation, it is affixed to the unbelievers who cannot enter the New Jerusalem (22:15). Cats fare a little better than dogs simply because they are not mentioned at all in Scripture and only briefly in the apocrypha. Perhaps the Hebrew nation avoided cats because Egyptians worshiped them ("Animals"). When we consider the great number of children in this world who go to bed every night hungry and unprotected and when we consider the great number of souls hungry for hope and unprotected from the wiles of the devil, perhaps our money can be better spent elsewhere. Although food and health care should be provided for our animals, we need to be careful to use the resources provided to us by our Master in an expedient way with the right priorities in mind.

• **Animals Teach Us.** God does intend, however, for us to observe animals and learn from their behavior. Job was told,

> But now ask the beasts, and they will teach you;
> And the birds of the air, and they will tell you;
> Or speak to the earth, and it will teach you;
> And the fish of the sea will explain to you.
> Who among all these does not know
> That the hand of the Lord has done this,
> In whose hand is the life of every living thing,
> And the breath of all mankind? (12:7-10)

We ascertain here that we should learn from animals and that God is in control, not only of our lives but also of the lives of every creature placed under our dominion on earth. Although we can pollute His streams, spout our carbon emissions into His air, waste His resources, and ultimately harm both our lives and the lives of every being on His earth, He is still ultimately the Overseer of His creation. We have little understanding of how or why the natural world and animals function as they do, and when we, with all our scientific reasoning, try to explain nature and instinctive behavior, we are often left confounded. Proverbs 30:18-19 says, "There are three things which are too wonderful for me, Yes, four which I do not understand: The way of an eagle in the air, The way of a serpent on a rock, The way of a ship in the midst of the sea, And the way of a man with a virgin." We have only to read what God told Job from the whirlwind in Job 38 and 39 to be overwhelmed by God's power and His intricate, well-ordered plan. We are no match in strength or wisdom to God and His creation. We can stand only in awe and learn from His Word.

Animals are used as both positive and negative examples in the Bible, and interestingly, the same animal may be presented in both lights at various times. For example, Christ is called both the Lion of Judah to show His nobility and strength "to open the scroll and to loose its seven seals" and the slain Lamb, worthy to be worshiped with a new song (Revelation 5:5-6). In other scriptures the lion's ferocious roar is used to describe a wicked ruler to be feared (Proverbs 28:15), and the sheep is a dumb animal easily lost (Isaiah 53:6). Depending upon the lesson and point of view, an animal's traits are subject to interpretation.

An assortment of birds and their behaviors are used multiple times in the Bible to teach various lessons, especially when they are correlated with similar actions in human beings. For example, how many times do we curse or speak ill of someone when we have no cause for doing so? Students often grumble about teachers who expect them to study; workers often criticize bosses who require them to carry out their duties in an expedient manner; and teens perpetually complain about concerned and vigilant parents who want to know who their companions are and where the teens are going. Proverbs 26:2 tells us such complaints, or curses, without cause never produce any good because they are like the flitting sparrow or a flying swallow. Being unfounded and without impact, they are merely empty words. However, we are warned to be careful about our criticism of those in power: "Do not curse the king, even in your thought; Do not curse the rich, even in your bedroom; For a bird of the air may carry your voice, And a bird in flight may tell the matter" (Ecclesiastes 10:20). Many an employee or politician has found himself the victim of those who would report his misspoken words. At times, "the air may carry [his] voice" through his own doing: consider the tapes recorded in the oval office of President Richard Nixon at his own request.

Sometimes we think too highly of ourselves when actually we are not wise at all, especially when we do not carry our plans through to their rightful conclusion. This type of behavior is like the ostrich – the largest bird on earth – who has no fear of the horse or rider because of her size. Yet, for all her pride and the waving of her wings, "she leaves her eggs on the ground, And warms them in the dust; She forgets that a foot may crush them, Or that a wild beast may break them" (Job 39:14-15). Her labor, we are told, is in vain, and so is ours when we hurriedly and haphazardly initiate our work without seeing it through to its appropriate end. The world is full of starters but has few finishers. Perhaps the ostrich syndrome best describes those who start their Christian life with enthusiasm but fail, for whatever reason, to continue a lifelong commitment. They may have gotten sidetracked and like "a partridge that broods but does not hatch," may have chased after riches that were not theirs by right (Jeremiah 17:11) when they should have pursued the treasure that lasts forever. The writer of Proverbs asks, "Will you set your eyes on that which is not? For riches certainly make themselves wings; They fly away like an eagle toward heaven" (23:5).

Even insects have important lessons to teach us. The ant, in particular, stands as an example to those who are not diligent workers or who do not plan ahead: "Go to the ant, you sluggard! consider her ways and be wise, Which, having no captain, Overseer or ruler, Provides her supplies in the summer, And gathers her food in the harvest" (Proverbs 6:6-8). The ant, the locust and the spider also make the "wise creature list" in Proverbs 30: the ant for its preparation and planning ahead despite its lack of strength; the locust for its group participation despite the lack of leadership; and the spider (lizard in some translations) for living in kings' palaces because of its skillful hands (30:24-28). Planning ahead and diligence are keys to success.

Various other animal analogies are notable as lessons. Wine that sparkles in the cup "bites like a serpent, And stings like a viper" (Proverbs 23:31-32). In Bible times water was mixed with wine for two reasons: (1) to purify the water, and (2) to weaken the wine. Historical records tell us of this practice in the early church when the Lord's Supper was served (Ferguson). Becoming involved with a fool and his folly, we are told in another analogy, is worse than meeting "a bear robbed of her cubs" (17:12). Too often, good but unwise people have been pulled into illegal schemes or scams that have either robbed them of their good name or their life savings. We are also cautioned about signing a note to help someone secure a loan, making ourselves financially liable: "My son, if you become surety for your friend, ... Deliver yourself like a gazelle from the hand of the hunter, And like a bird from the hand of the fowler" (6:1, 5). Sometimes a humorous or ridiculous analogy is used; a personal favorite is the one attached to a beautiful, but indiscreet, woman who is like "a ring of gold in a swine's snout" (11:22).

Faithful followers of the Lord can find comfort in many scripture similes despite those Christ used to warn His disciples: "Behold, I send you out as sheep in the midst of wolves. Therefore be wise as serpents and harmless as doves" (Matthew 10:16). Happily, we are told in Isaiah 40:31 that "those who wait on the Lord Shall renew their strength; They shall mount up with wings like eagles, They shall run and not be weary, They shall walk and not faint." Perhaps most comforting is the peaceful kingdom we are promised in heaven, described figuratively in Isaiah 11:6-9 and reminiscent of the innocence and tranquility of the Garden of Eden before sin entered the world:

> The wolf also shall dwell with the lamb,
> The leopard shall lie down with the young goat,
> The calf and the young lion and the fatling together;
> And a little child shall lead them.
> The cow and the bear shall graze;
> Their young ones shall lie down together;
> And the lion shall eat straw like the ox.
> The nursing child shall play by the cobra's hole,
> And the weaned child shall put his hand in the viper's den.
> They shall not hurt nor destroy in all My holy mountain,
> For the earth shall be full of the knowledge of the Lord
> As the waters cover the sea. (Isaiah 11:6-9)

Shod With the Preparation of the Gospel

1. Read Job 38–39. Discuss both the forces of nature and the instinctive behavior of the animals and the way they proclaim God's power.
2. Why do some people believe that animals have souls and will go to heaven or hell in the afterlife? Research the scriptures people use to support this belief (i.e., Genesis 9:5, Isaiah 11:6-9) and discuss.
3. Can you think of an example of someone in the Bible having a household pet? (Hint: See an Old Testament parable.)

little ewe lamb.

4. America's favorite household pet is vilified in the Bible. Read and discuss these figurative applications: Deuteronomy 23:18; 1 Samuel 17:43; 2 Samuel 9:8; Psalm 22:20; Matthew 7:6; 2 Peter 2:22.
5. Examine these New Testament animal analogies: Luke 13:32; Matthew 23:37; Matthew 25:32-33; 1 Peter 5:8; Matthew 6:19; Luke 11:12.
6. Should animals be used in medical research?

Chapter 12

Finding Our FOCUS

"I will pray with the spirit, and I will also pray with the understanding. I will sing with the spirit, and I will also sing with the understanding."
(1 Corinthians 14:15)

Barefoot With Dolly

When I was 6 years old, my mom and dad decided to become semi-missionaries. Until then, we worshiped at the Ethridge church where my great-grandfather had served as one of the first elders in the late 1800s and where my dad was serving at the time as an elder. I hated to make the move and leave behind my wonderful Bible school teacher, Miss Annie.

The Ethridge church met in a two-story, white-block building next door to our general merchandise store. It had a steep flight of concrete steps leading up to the double front doors. Since we had no upstairs at home, I loved to play on these steps by running up and down, which sometimes got me in trouble with Mother and her endless supply of switches. Inside were unpadded, wooden pews, enough to seat 150 worshipers, facing a large stage that held an ornately carved pulpit. Overhead was a bead board ceiling with globe lights suspended on black chains. The block walls and wooden ceiling, floor and pews amplified the singing, making it, if not the best, the loudest in the county.

We left Ethridge to begin worshiping at Sims Ridge, a little country congregation truly in the backwoods. What a contrast! When we first began attending there, we met in an old unpainted, clapboard building that had been abandoned years before. It had rough pine benches with no backs and a pot-bellied wood stove at the center front. Its stove pipe ascended several feet before bending in an elbow to exhaust the smoke out the back wall. This meant that the preacher had to stand behind and under this pipe to deliver his lessons; while he sweated in the winter, the 10 or 12 of us who were listening froze. Old Brother Coleman served as both preacher and song leader. He loved to sing "The Lily of the Valley," and it quickly became my favorite.

After about a year, we switched to the schoolhouse on the other side of the graveyard. It was in better condition. The clapboard was painted, the floor was solid, and a gas-fed heater radiated warmth at the front. We soon exchanged old student desks for slatted pews and improved the lighting. The attendance went up to 25 or so, and Brother Teddy Crews began preaching every second and fifth Sunday. He had a lisp that was distracting, but he had a gentle, good heart.

To get to Sims Ridge we had to drive 22 miles, the last 13 on a rough, unpaved road with steep hills and sharp curves. (One time my dad braked on a deeply slanted curve, and we collided with an oncoming car.) Two creeks without bridges had to be forded. One was deep and wide with a particularly rough bottom. If it rained hard on Saturday night, we were forced to detour by Piney, adding another 10 miles to the trip. I kept up with certain landmarks on the regular route – the Houser Cemetery, the Pea Ridge church, my Aunt Dixie's house, and the wide creek – to know how much farther the trip would be.

Our family rarely traveled this road alone. After a couple of years, we began transporting young preachers from David Lipscomb College to speak at Sims Ridge. They would arrive in Ethridge on the Greyhound bus from Nashville, and we would take them to church in our car, bring them home, feed them lunch, and put them back on the bus on Sunday afternoon. Many preachers, some of them foreign, got their start at Sims Ridge. From my dad's point of view, room was still available in his automobile, so we would pick up riders along the way. In my younger years, a mother and her teenage son and daughter rode with us; in later years, we regularly carried four small children and their mother. At various times other people joined our entourage. Needless to say, the car was crowded with people crammed to the front and back of the seats – sometimes on top, sometimes underneath someone else.

The ultimate hazard of attending church in the country was the wasp attacks. Because we had no air conditioning, the windows of the schoolhouse had to be opened, which allowed all kinds of insects to enter during worship. Worst of all were the huge, red wasps that circled overhead all during the service. Every spring they swarmed, entering not only through the windows, but from every crack or crevice where they had spent the winter. I worshiped in mortal fear, but not of the Lord. Often, a wasp would swing down to light on a song book, a Bible or the bench nearby. Most of the time we would sit very still, hoping it would fly elsewhere. At times, the songbooks and Bibles were our only weapons to smash the ugly creatures. Worst of all was when a wasp lit on someone. Although an onlooker might have surmised that the worshiper had suddenly been filled with the Holy Spirit, it was only a dance to remove the offending insect with its threatening stinger.

Wasps, as well as black widow spiders, were also a threat if a trip to the bathroom could not be avoided. Behind the church building was an outhouse, the only facility available. I dreaded "having to go." First, I watched for snakes lurking in the weeds along the path. Then I opened the creaking door to look fearfully overhead for wasp nests and spiderwebs. I was also afraid someone else would need to go at the same time and would either see me through the cracks or open the door, which was latched by a cotton string looped over a nail.

How much actual worshiping we did at Sims Ridge under these conditions I do not know. I remember little of what I heard from the pulpit, but I do remember the fear. Surely, God in His mercy would overlook my straying mind while I was under attack by one of His creatures.

Rest a Spell

1. What are some of your earliest memories of worship? Did you have a special Bible school teacher or older mentor?
2. If you grew up in a denominational church with a different style of worship than you experience now, share some of the practices you observed.

3. What distracted you during worship as you were growing up? What distracts you during worship now?
4. How much entertainment and what types of entertainment should parents provide for their children who are present during worship?
5. Why do many people prefer sitting in back pews at worship whereas others prefer sitting toward the front?
6. Should worship be more entertaining?

Walking With the Master

The members of a church rejoiced when a certain gentleman responded to the gospel and was baptized. After witnessing his immersion in the baptistry that was constructed in the wall behind and above the pulpit, the congregation rose to sing a hymn of praise while he made his way up the steps from the water. As they sang, he realized his mistake – he had gone to the wrong side, the one leading to the ladies' dressing room. Rather than wade across and disturb the worship, he chose to swim underwater, forgetting, of course, the glass front that made him visible to the entire congregation (Wilhelm 90). No doubt, this humorous spectacle distracted every worshiper from the hymn being addressed to God.

We have all been distracted from worship probably more times than we would like to admit. Things happen. Whether it be feedback in a microphone, a child embarrassing his mother with a temper fit, a dropped communion tray, or a misspoken word or phrase, some irregularity has interrupted our focus on worship in the assembly. However, a momentary break in concentration differs greatly from the continuous practice of disengaging our hearts and minds from the acts of corporate worship. We must be careful that we do not find ourselves in an automatic mode, giving only lip service to the Lord or speaking rashly in worship while letting our hearts "utter anything hastily before God." Rather, we must ensure that we "draw near to hear rather than to give the sacrifice of fools" (Ecclesiastes 5:1-2).

Perhaps it is more difficult today than ever before for us to maintain our focus. We are so bombarded by excessive stimulation through modern technology that our senses rebel at the idea of an hour that demands our full and undivided attention in a quiet environment where "all things

[are] done decently and in order" (1 Corinthians 14:40). Attention spans have become so short that we find ourselves "multitasking" during sermons and prayers. We want a commercial break, a quick trip to the refrigerator, or an activity that requires physical movement. Even sitting quietly and meditating on Christ's sacrifice as we partake of His body and blood become more difficult because we are so sensory dependent. For this reason, many congregations have added "white noise" (music) to mask the stillness. Silence has become truly deafening in our society today because there is so little of it; in fact, it is practically impossible to experience absolute silence or even silence punctuated only by sounds emanating from natural sources (i.e., bird song, wind soughing through pines). Yet Zechariah says, "Be silent, all flesh, before the Lord, for He is aroused from His holy habitation!" (2:13).

When we gather together, we must remain cognizant of Christ's presence with us (Matthew 18:20) and of God the Father who is the object of our worship (James 4:8). The Hebrews writer reminds us that we must "serve God acceptably with reverence and godly fear. For our God is a consuming fire" (12:28-29). Surely, if we are aware that the divine Godhead is present in our assemblies, that awareness will change our attitudes and actions. We will engage our hearts and minds, knowing that God hears our thoughts perhaps more loudly than He hears the words on our lips. We hope it cannot be said of us as it was in Isaiah's day: "These people draw near to Me with their mouth, And honor Me with their lips, But their heart is far from Me" (Isaiah 29:13; Matthew 15:8). Rather, like David, we should be able to say, "I will praise You with my whole heart" (Psalm 138:1).

We must also distinguish between the mode of worship commanded by God in the Old Testament and the worship commanded of New Testament Christians. Although the Old Testament serves as symbol and archetype of the New Testament, it was transformed from elaborate rituals in a gold-adorned temple to simplified acts possible for worshipers in any rudimentary situation. Such worship is not dependent upon rules or rituals, tabernacles or temples; rather, it is dependent upon willing obedience from a heart of love. The temple made with hands has been replaced with our bodies that now serve as "the temple of the Holy Spirit" (1 Corinthians 6:19) and "as living stones ... being built up a spiritual house" of which Christ is the cornerstone (1 Peter 2:5-6). The sacrifice of unblemished animals has been replaced "through the offering of the body of Jesus Christ once for all" (Hebrews 10:10). Neither do we need Levitical priests to perform our acts of devotion for us because we are now "a holy priesthood" (1 Peter 2:5). The worship of the first Christians is expressed simply: "they continued steadfastly in the apostles' doctrine and fellowship, in the breaking of bread, and in prayers" (Acts 2:42). When we look at the apostolic examples of worship given throughout the New Testament, we find the acts of corporate worship were expressed in preaching (Acts 20:7; 1 Corinthians 1:17-18), singing (Ephesians 5:19; Colossians 3:16), praying (Philippians 4:6; Acts 2:42), partaking of the Lord's Supper (Acts 20:7; 1 Corinthians 10:16-17), and giving (1 Corinthians 16:1-2; 2 Corinthians 9:6-7). When we do what they did, we get what they got – simple New Testament worship. John Price, in his book *Old Light on New Worship,* says,

> The unconverted man and much of the modern professing church will enter a gospel worship service containing nothing more than the simple ordinances of the New Testament and declare it all dull and uninteresting. They will have contempt upon its simplicity and plainness. But they disdain such services only because they cannot discern the glorious spiritual realities that are taking place by faith. We must not be troubled or perplexed by this. We must not be ashamed of the simplicity of our worship because carnal men cannot see its true glory. Men will never find the simplicity of gospel worship attractive apart from the power of the Holy Spirit in their hearts. (214)

When we put too much emphasis on our surroundings – vaulted architecture, stained-glass windows, rich fabrics and furnishings – and are more concerned with the entertainment factor – drama, choral groups, animated PowerPoints, DVDs, musical instruments – in our worship, we are in danger of distorting the spiritual house that God has built. As the kingdom of heaven (Matthew 3:2), it belongs to God: it is spiritual, not physical; it is heavenly, not earthly (John 18:36; Romans 14:17). "It is not concerned with real estate, a literal throne, or an earthly reign. It is not a social club. It is not an entertainment medium. ...

It is the rule of God in the hearts of men" (Chesser 243).

If we have become like the priests of Malachi's day who despised God's name by offering unworthy sacrifices (Malachi 1:6-7) and who found worship to be a "weariness" (v. 13), perhaps we are not truly converted. Rather, as mature Christians we should have the attitude of David who says, "I was glad when they said to me, 'Let us go into the house of the Lord' " (Psalm 122:1). Such an attitude toward worship requires preparation of the heart and the mind. In fact, it is impossible to worship acceptably without both preparation and continuous practice.

• **Preparation.** We cannot be just "Sunday-go-to-meeting" Christians. Preparation for worship begins with a daily life devoted to personal study and prayer and to good deeds. First of all, we must allow God to speak to us each day through His Word. Timothy was instructed: "Be diligent to present yourself approved to God, a worker who does not need to be ashamed, rightly dividing the word of truth" (2 Timothy 2:15). Without a firsthand knowledge of God's Word, we have no way to "test the spirits, whether they are of God" (1 John 4:1) or to recognize "savage wolves [who] will come in among you, not sparing the flock" (Acts 20:29).

Along with daily Bible study, we are to "pray without ceasing, in every thing [giving] thanks" (1 Thessalonians 5:17-18). The necessity of praying privately was first addressed by Christ Himself who said, "But you, when you pray, go into your room, and when you have shut your door, pray to your Father who is in the secret place; and your Father who sees in secret will reward you openly" (Matthew 6:6).

Meanwhile, we must be Christ's hands and feet on earth, going about doing "good to all, especially to those who are of the household of faith" (Galatians 6:10). John asks, "But whoever has this world's goods, and sees his brother in need, and shuts up his heart from him, how does the love of God abide in him?" (1 John 3:17). Through these daily acts of study, prayer and benevolence, we prepare ourselves to enter before the throne of God on the first day of the week to worship with a pure heart.

Before entering the assembly, however, we must tend to practical matters as well. We cannot sleep as late as possible on Sunday mornings, hastily bathe and dress, grab a quick breakfast, and drive at breakneck speed expecting to be in a calm, worshipful mood when we arrive at the meeting place. Nor can we bicker with our children over which clothes to wear, hunt frantically for our lost Bibles that we have not used since the last church meeting, or fight with our husband about his or our tardiness. Such Sunday morning scenarios are played out in many Christian families, much to their detriment and that of the congregation where they attend. Tardiness to worship is a symptom of soul sickness. Although we would never arrive late at work for fear of being fired, we sometimes treat the Lord and our church family as unworthy of our concern – as if worship were merely a leisure-time activity (although we are never too late to get good seats at a sporting or theatrical event)! We slide into our usual back-row pew as we try to catch up on the announcements we missed or on the second stanza of the opening hymn. Correctly defined, tardiness is arriving after or at the appointed time; being "on time" is actually arriving 10 minutes early. Obviously, preparation for worship involves planning and forethought as well as dedication to the Lord.

• **Continuous Practice.** Continuous practice is also necessary for acceptable worship. We are weakened by disconnecting ourselves from the family of God. We must assemble with other saints both to give and receive the benefits intended for us as members of Christ's body. How can we "esteem others better than [ourselves]" or look out "for the interests of others" (Philippians 2:3-4) if we do not see each other on a regular basis? How can we "consider one another in order to stir up love and good works" if we forsake "the assembling of ourselves together" (Hebrews 10:24-25)? How can we "hold fast the confession of our hope without wavering" (v. 23) or exhort one another (v. 25)? And, how can we focus on worshiping the Lord if we are not even present?

Meeting with the saints is commanded, but we should want to assemble with our brothers and sisters in Christ because we love God and desire Him more than anything on earth. The attitude of David, the man after God's own heart, stands as our example when he says, "As the deer pants for the water brooks, So pants my soul for You, O God. My soul thirsts for God, for the living God" (Psalm 42:1-2). Later he states, "How lovely is Your tabernacle, O Lord of hosts! My soul longs, yes, even faints For the courts of the Lord; My heart and my flesh cry out for the living

God" (84:1-2). Such a passionate desire for worship emanates only from a humble, obedient heart. As an extra motivation, parents and mature Christians have the added obligation of teaching and being worthy examples to the young. David says, "One generation shall praise Your works to another, And shall declare Your mighty acts" (145:4). No scripture more clearly expresses the need to teach our children by both example and word than that found in Deuteronomy 6, when God commanded,

> You shall love the Lord your God with all your heart, with all your soul, and with all your strength. And these words which I command you today shall be in your heart. You shall teach them diligently to your children, and shall talk of them when you sit in your house, when you walk by the way, when you lie down, and when you rise up. You shall bind them as a sign on your hand, and they shall be as frontlets between your eyes. You shall write them on the doorposts of your house and on your gates. (6:5-9)

We serve as examples, either for good or for ill. More often than not, if we offer vain worship and have lax attitudes toward our commitment to God and His worship assembly, our children will follow after us. If we put the things of this world before Him, so will they. Christ said, "But whoever causes one of these little ones who believe in Me to stumble, it would be better for him if a millstone were hung around his neck, and he were thrown into the sea" (Mark 9:42).

• **Staying Focused.** Because our worship is so important, not only to us but to those who imitate us, we must be focused. After preparing our hearts and minds daily for a meaningful and scriptural worship, we can help ourselves stay focused while worshiping by finding what works best for us. Here are some suggestions for keeping our hearts and minds in sync with our lips as we worship in the assembly.

Before Worship Begins. Spend some quiet moments focusing on the purpose for being in the assembly. Silently read a favorite passage, pray or think through the blessings of the previous week. Even in the midst of the fellowship and visiting going on around us, we can quietly withdraw a few moments before worship begins to prepare for what is about to occur.

Public Reading of God's Word. If the version being used for the scripture reading is not available to follow in print or on a screen, we can use our personal Bibles and note the differences in word choices and phrases used to express the same meaning in the different versions. A study Bible is useful, giving us a chance to glance at the notes accompanying the passage for more insight.

Congregational Singing. This is the one activity in which we all participate orally – we must sing; it is commanded (Ephesians 5:19; Colossians 3:16). If the song is unfamiliar, we can at least quietly say the words. If the song is so familiar that our minds automatically go into hibernation, a freshness can be brought to the lyrics by thinking: What would these words mean to a new Christian? What would I think if I were hearing these words for the first time? If losing the sense of the words is a common problem, we can prepare for worship by reading the life experiences that prompted the lyricists to write them. Books such as Kenneth W. Osbeck's *One Hundred Hymn Stories* and *One Hundred More Hymn Stories* will help us gain further insight.

The Collection. Although putting money or a check in the collection plate may not feel like worship, it is. We can make it even more so by thanking God silently for all the blessings, both physical and spiritual, experienced during the past week, ticking them off one by one. When we do so, we should easily be able to give bountifully with a cheerful heart (2 Corinthians 9:1-7).

Preaching. Not all sermons are created equal. No matter how poorly it may be presented, we can find points that will make us grow as Christians. Taking notes, preferably in a journal, will help us maintain our attention. Checking the notes in a study Bible to gain more information is helpful. We really are capable of multitasking in our thoughts during a sermon, but those thoughts should be adding to, not detracting from, the message. If we find ourselves in a situation where we simply cannot hear what the speaker is saying, a rare event indeed, then we can substitute Bible reading for the message.

Public Prayer. Not every man is accomplished at leading public prayer, even though he may pray often privately. The responsibility of leading the thoughts of everyone in the congregation along the same thought paths can be daunting for some. For that reason, many prayer leaders fall into the trap of repetitive phraseology that, when overused, holds little or no meaning. As silent participants we can add to the meaning of the public prayer by our own additions (i.e., specific names of people who are sick or bereaved or who need to obey the gospel). God easily hears all of us; He "knows the things you have need of before you ask Him" (Matthew 6:8). And what we or the public leader cannot express well is taken care of by "the Spirit [who] also helps in our weaknesses" and "makes intercession for us with groanings which cannot be uttered" (Romans 8:26). The important thing is that we actually pray, not plan our Sunday meal or after-church activities during worship.

The Lord's Supper. Although all worshipful acts in corporate worship are necessary, we cannot deny that the most important act is the Lord's Supper: it was the primary purpose for which New Testament Christians came together (Acts 20:7). This act truly makes us one (1 Corinthians 10:16-17). Paul gave special instruction and correction to the church at Corinth who were profaning the Lord's Supper (11:20-30). To focus on worldly things while partaking of Christ's body is the ultimate sacrilege. Special care must be taken to center our hearts and minds on His sacrifice, "For he who eats and drinks in an unworthy manner eats and drinks judgment to himself, not discerning the Lord's body" (v. 29). Communing with Him during this time is personal; for this reason, the imposition of singing while partaking of the emblems can be distracting and, therefore, should be avoided. Each Christian must find his/her own focus, whether it be through prayerful images of the cross-borne sacrifice replayed in the mind, a silent recitation of the meaningful words of a hymn about the death of Christ, or reflection on scriptures such as Isaiah 53 or Matthew 27:27-54. The important thing is that we truly worship our Savior during this period of time.

In all that we do in our corporate worship, we must make sure that we are in accordance with the type of worship prescribed in the New Testament, both by command and apostolic example, and that we are not offering vain worship by following traditions of men with an empty heart. What seems so pleasing to us may not, after all, be pleasing to God. As Peter reminds us:

> And if you call on the Father, who without partiality judges according to each one's work, conduct yourselves through-

out the time of your stay here in fear; knowing that you were not redeemed with corruptible things, like silver or gold, from your aimless conduct received by tradition from your fathers, but with the precious blood of Christ, as of a lamb without blemish and without spot. (1 Peter 1:17-19)

Shod With the Preparation of the Gospel

1. Share with others personal practices that help you stay focused during the various acts of worship.
2. Why is it important to pray for one another in the public assembly? See James 5:16. Relate an incident in which you have seen the results of prayer.
3. What hymn choices do you find more conducive to worship? Share with others a hymn or hymns that have particular meaning to you.
4. How can we prevent worship that is performed "decently and in order" from becoming tradition bound?
5. Should we provide alternative activities for children outside the formal worship of the church? Why or why not? At what ages could such activities be appropriate?
6. Read 1 Timothy 2:8-15 and discuss the role of women in the public assembly.
7. Make a list of suggestions for improving the worshipful nature of the public assembly in your congregation. You may want to present a composite list to your elders for consideration.

Chapter 13

"Make a joyful noise unto the Lord, all ye lands. Serve the Lord with gladness: Come before His presence with singing."
(Psalm 100:1-2 KJV)

Barefoot With Dolly

My greatest ambition growing up was to be a star in a Hollywood musical. I wanted a beautiful soprano voice like Jane Powell or Doris Day or at least a nice contralto one like Rosemary Clooney. I wanted to dance, too, so I practiced walking on my toes across the entire length of our living room floor. I could picture myself floating across the Technicolor screen with Fred Astaire or Gower Champion like Ginger Rogers and Marge Champion, or hoofing it like Ann Miller. They were my heroes.

Unfortunately, dance lessons weren't readily available in a small country town, and I was a mediocre singer at best. I blame my genetic make-up for this lack of talent. Although my dad was a fairly good bass who couldn't read music, my mother never audibly sang in church. Although she claimed to have once played the piano, I never saw her actually perform. She did, however, insist that my brother and I take lessons.

Mrs. Walton taught both of us. She had moved to our little Tennessee hamlet from Iowa and spoke in a strange tongue – Midwestern English. She also had a weird hairdo made up of twisted topknots held in place with plastic combs. Her neck plunged in a series of folds to the lacy collar of her dresses, which were printed with tiny flowers on thin cotton voile, worn even in winter under her three-quarter-length wool coat. She had a jolly laugh like Santa Claus and was the only person I knew who could play the violin. I loved her, but I didn't love practice.

Mrs. Walton would visit our home each week for a 30-minute lesson. She sat at the end of the keyboard tapping her fingers gently like a metronome to keep my rhythm even. Only if I showed acceptable progress during the week did I get one of her large gold stars on my music. Smaller blue and red stars marked minimal progress. We graduated from my first book of nursery rhyme tunes to more difficult songs and more intricate fingering. As the years passed, so did my enthusiasm. Daily practice went from 10 minutes to 30 minutes to an hour. My back hunched, my neck hurt, and my feet dangled to the floor. I was miserable.

My mother took her afternoon nap while I practiced. The bedroom alarm clock was set on top of the upright piano for me to keep up with the time. The minutes crept more slowly because I glanced up so often to see how much time had passed. It was then that I came up with what I thought was a clever plan. I simply moved the hands forward a little to cut off some of the practice time. After a while, my dad complained about how poorly his alarm clock was keeping correct time; he was arriving at the store for work much too early. My deception came to an end when one hour of practice passed so quickly that my mother got only 10 minutes of naptime.

Recitals were a yearly affair, scheduled at the local Methodist church where a piano and ample seating were available. My favorite recital pieces were "Mountain Shower" from *The Etude* music magazine that allowed me to trickle down three octaves of chromatic notes to emulate a lightning strike, and "The Green Cathedral," a recital standard. One year I played the monotonous "Moonlight Sonata" by Beethoven as accompaniment to Mrs. Walton's violin rendition of "Ave Maria."

It stands to reason that I was one decade out of sync with my peers who were gravitating toward rock and roll. I grew up listening to the music my brother played: Irving Berlin's "Alexander's Ragtime Band" and "Always," Stephen Foster's timeless tunes like "Beautiful Dreamer" and "Jeanie With the Light Brown Hair," and songs from World War II. I could sing all the words to "Coming in on a Wing and a Prayer," "My Buddy," "I'll Be Seeing You," and "Goodnight, Irene." When I received a record player for Christmas, my first purchase was a 33⅓ vinyl record of Glenn Miller's big band music from the soundtrack of *The Glenn Miller Story.*

Despite the piano lessons and musical interests, my singing and dancing ambitions fizzled. Mother did sign me up for six weeks of tap dance, but I came down with the mumps and missed all but the first lesson. I sang solos on several local talent shows in elementary school, but because I sang old-fashioned songs, I never made it to the finals until I was 14. At that time I entered the Kiwanis Club's countywide talent show and sang the naughty "I Cain't Say No" from *Oklahoma* while accompanying myself on a ukulele. I won first prize, a TV performance on "Pride of the Volunteer State" on WSM-TV in Nashville. I'm sure the viewing audiences found the performance a gauche and amusing, if not downright hilarious, anomaly.

I knew nothing about country music and was not impressed when, through the 4-H club, I was invited to spend a weekend in Nashville to attend the Grand Ole Opry. We went backstage to meet some of the stars, but the only performers I had ever heard of were Minnie Pearl and the Jordanaires. We went to a country music star's home where I played chopsticks on the piano with Del Wood and Archie Campbell, but I didn't have the slightest idea who they were.

Rock and roll came of age in my preteen years, and my peers were learning the latest dance, the bop. To stay in the swing of things, so did I. Mike, the cowboy from our primary grades, became Mike the guitar player. Because I was learning to play the alto saxophone, we formed a band. He sang "Party Doll" with a backup group as he strummed, and I played melody. By this time, Elvis Presley had become a big star, and my mother and dad loaded me and several classmates in the car to go to Lawrenceburg to see him sing "Love Me Tender" in his first movie. All the girls in the Crockett Theater screamed throughout the entire performance.

In later years I would come to appreciate my musical experiences. Little did I know how important they were at the time. The music I came to appreciate was wide in scope, from opry to opera, from rock and roll combo to symphony orchestra. My life is still filled with music, but I am not a performer except in the place it counts most – as a worshiper of God playing on the strings of my heart.

Rest a Spell

1. What grand ambitions did you have as a child? How did those ambitions change as you grew older? What prompted the change?
2. Name some popular songs from when you were growing up. What is your favorite popular song today?
3. How important is music in your life today? Do you listen to music as you exercise or work?
4. Can you read music? If so, how did you learn? Are people who can't read music somewhat "illiterate"?
5. Are you aware of the music playing in stores when you are shopping? How much do you think that music affects you as a shopper?
6. What changes have you noticed in recent years in the hymns we sing in worship? What concerns, if any, do you have about these changes?
7. Is it important for children to take music lessons? Why are the arts the first programs cut in our schools when the budget is tight?

Walking With the Master

It was the dreaded half-hour of torture again. Brian would droop sadly like an old man on a park bench, his back rounded into a hump, his chin jutting toward his music. The piano bench was too high, even for an over-tall 8-year-old; the toes of his blue sneakers could barely graze the hardwood floor. His concentration was fierce. Settling his hands on the keys, he would line each finger up carefully with its home key. Long dark lashes would bounce up and down as he glanced first at the notes, then at the keyboard, translating symbol to sound. With each mistake, he would begin again like a scratched record, the finale floating in infinity. Amazingly, a melody would somehow begin to emerge from the jumble of notes, and his thumbs would no longer duel in mortal combat over middle C. When time was up, he would tumble from the stool with a whoop of joy, miraculously transforming the old man of the piano to a boisterous boy. With shoelaces flying, he would dash for freedom, a blur of fast-forward motion.

Both of our sons were less than enthusiastic when I insisted that they take piano lessons. However, my motives were clear. Because I could read music, I considered anyone who could not only semi-illiterate. I wanted both sons to be able to sing bass or tenor as adults, and I knew the piano was the best way for them to learn to read notes. Never did I expect them to be pianists, and neither of them is, although both play guitars for their own amusement quite skillfully as adults. Ultimately, however, both of them can easily sing harmony in worship to the Lord.

Little did I know, however, what other wonderful perks would come from learning to play an instrument – actual God-blessed bonuses built into the brains of all children who actively experience music.

• **Educational Value of Music.** Several scientific studies have noted that playing music on an instrument, in particular on a keyboard, has great educational value. In fact, "intensive practice of an instrument leads to discernible enlargement of parts of the cerebral cortex, the layer of gray matter most closely associated with higher brain function" ("Music"), resulting in improvement of spatial reasoning, reading ability, verbal memory and mathematical skill, all of which have been demonstrated in various scientific studies involving students. For example, several studies with 4- to 5-year-olds show that the more musical skill children have, "the greater their degree of phonological awareness and reading development" (Sousa). Also, after six months of piano training, children in one study scored 34 percent higher on spatial-temporal reasoning tests (Sousa).

Keyboard practice also increases the ability to understand fractions in mathematics. Second graders from low socio-economic backgrounds in Los Angeles were given four months of piano lessons, resulting in a 166 percent higher score on proportional mathematics tests. Interestingly, this type of math is usually not introduced until the fifth or sixth grades. In another study, 90 boys ages 6 to 15 were given memory tests. The half who had participated in the school's strings program for one to five years demonstrated higher verbal memory. Even those who had chosen to drop out of the program retained their gains when tested a year later (Sousa).

Music education can also level the academic playing field for the disadvantaged. In another California study using low socio-economic students, researchers found that continuous music lessons during the high school years reaped significantly higher academic scores, including doubling mathematics scores and increasing social studies scores by 40 percent (Sousa). All of these studies confirm the disservice we do our children when music programs are among the first budget cuts we make in our public school systems.

Listening to music, although not as powerful as performing on a musical instrument, has some educational value as well. Although playing classical music for an infant will probably not produce a little Einstein, a 1993 study did find that "the ability to form mental images from physical objects or see patterns in time and space" improved in college students after they listened to 10 minutes of Mozart. However, "The Mozart Effect," as it was called, disappeared quickly and did not result in higher IQs. Since that time, other studies have confirmed that listening to Mozart and similar classical music by other composers does improve the ability to sequence or reassemble objects. This knowledge is useful to educators who can use passive listening in the classroom to enhance certain types of learning activities (Sousa).

• **Emotional Response to Music.** It is no surprise that music also appeals to our emotions, affecting us physically. Who among us has not been uplifted by the purloined warbling of a mockingbird or the more predictable trilling of the bird from which he stole the song? Nothing is more cheerful than these musical musings from God's winged creations, accompanied by the tympani of water trickling over rocks in a forest stream. Although scientists do not understand the connection between emotion and music, studies definitively correlate them. Slow tempos and minor keys produce sadness that in turn slows our pulse, raises our blood pressure, and lowers our body temperature. Music with rapid notes written in a major key can produce a happy feeling that results in faster breathing. Dissonant chords and non-melodic music, so prevalent in modern classical works and in hard rock, increase pulse rates and may induce fear or unpleasant emotions ("Biology"). "[T]here is some indication that music can affect levels of various hormones, including cortisol (involved in arousal and stress), testosterone (aggression and arousal) and oxytocin (nurturing behavior) as well as trigger release of the natural opiates known as endorphins" ("Music").

Although the 17th-century poet William Congreve knew nothing about endorphins, he surely was correct when he surmised that "Music hath charms to soothe a savage breast, / To soften rocks, or bend a knotted oak" (Congreve). In 1 Samuel we are told that David's skill on the harp relieved Saul from the evil spirit that tormented him after the Spirit of God left him (16:14-23). We can use music to our advantage as well today to help us alleviate the stresses that come in to our daily lives. Some hospitals even use music to "speed a patient's healing and relax someone who is nervous about undergoing major medical work" (Jennings). Meanwhile, nursing homes play quiet music at meal times to stimulate the appetites of patients, and many businesses pep up the office environment with light jazz in the afternoons to reenergize their employees (Jennings).

Because music can subtly control our emotions and actions in both the work place and in commerce, we need to be both conscious and wary of its power to manipulate our emotional responses. For example, when shopping during the Christmas holidays, we must not succumb to the happy tunes, accompanied by flashing lights and bright colors, that tempt us to spend more than we have in our bank accounts.

Few forces are more powerful than music. It can make people smile, cry, fight or fall in love. It can influence people to drink Coca-Cola, vote Republican, or drive a Chevrolet. It's a language that needs no interpreter. Regardless of whether the motivation is to heal listeners or make the musician rich, music has a unique capability to affect people's lives profoundly (Gill, Rotondi and Obrecht).

Ultimately, music can dupe us by producing emotional responses that we may misinterpret. This is especially true in the spiritual realm. Although the "essence of spirituality is an awareness of a higher form of inspiration," that heightened state we feel and attribute to a religious experience can also be produced without religion. "Concentrating, focusing, and listening, which are requirements for becoming a good musician, are necessary for exploring the inner being" and "the act of playing is a form of meditation that allows separation from thought" (Gill, Rotondi and Obrecht). Musicians often describe this as a "die sensation" or "becoming the instrument." One professional guitarist, Martin Simpson, recalls such a transcendental experience while playing a concert in England when he felt as if he were suspended in air above the stage watching himself play. Audiences can also experience such transcendental moments where they too feel "spiritually" enlightened in their emotional response (Gill, Rotondi and Obrecht).

• **Dangers of Instrumental Music in Worship.** Herein lies the danger of using instruments in our worship to God, for the listener can be so caught up in the emotional response to soaring violins (associated too with romance), the pulsating bass rhythms (echoed in the resonant ribcage where our heart resides), and the uplifting melodies played on an organ or piano that he may falsely attribute his "awareness of a higher form of inspiration" to the wrong source. "Religion may help a person achieve a heightened state of spirituality, but a person can be spiritual without being religious" (Gill, Rotondi, and Obrecht). It is, perhaps, for this reason that there is no record of instrumentation in the first-century church worship. God wants our words of praise to overflow from both our understanding and our hearts: "What is the conclusion then? I will pray with the spirit, and I will also pray with the understanding. I will sing with the spirit, and I will also sing with the understanding" (1 Corinthians 14:15).

Although specific instruments were allowed in temple worship under the Old Law, Christian worship found its basis in synagogue worship in which no instruments were used (Price 68-69). The purpose of music in the New Testament church is best expressed in Colossians 3:16: "Let the word of Christ dwell in you richly in all wisdom, teaching and admonishing one another in psalms and hymns and spiritual songs, singing with grace in your hearts to the Lord." And again, in Ephesians 5:18-21: "[B]e filled with the Spirit, speaking to one another in psalms and hymns and spiritual songs, singing and making melody in your heart to the Lord, giving thanks always for all things to God the Father in the name of our Lord Jesus Christ, submitting to one another in the fear of God." Any musical noise, no matter how beautiful it may be, should not interfere with the clear expression of words of praise that can be easily comprehended by other worshipers and by God.

As many modern religious groups assemble today, it is increasingly more difficult to distinguish what they term "worship" from a rock concert. The instruments include electronic keyboards, guitars and drums, sometimes backed with a whole orchestra. Theatrical lighting shines upon backup singers who gyrate to the throbbing beat. A featured singer repeats a single phrase to build his listeners to a "heightened state," and an audience waves their hands in similar fashion to rock fans with lighters. God is not a God of chaos but of order and design, and such worship is reminiscent of that performed at the foot of Mount Sinai around the golden calf when Joshua "heard the noise of the people as they shouted" and thought there was war in the camp (Exodus 32:17). The scene strikes no similarity at all to the worship of the New Testament church, nor to the worship that followed for the next 600 years (only two organs had been used in any church by the ninth century) (Price 84). Sometimes such a performance is so loud that, as occurred in one church building in my hometown, the speakers that were designed for a small organ and choir were blown out and had to be replaced.

Perhaps Jerome, a Greek scholar who lived at the end of the fourth century and totally rejected instruments in worship, said it best:

> Let young men hear this, let those hear it who have the office of singing in the church, that they sing not with their voice, but with their heart to the Lord; not like tragedians, physically preparing their throat and mouth, that they may sing after the fashion of the theatre in the church. He that has but an ill voice, if he has good works, is a sweet singer before God. (Price 192)

The music sung by all of us as "performers" before His heavenly throne in worship must be accompanied only by the strings of a pure heart, not for our entertainment but for the glory of God. Despite my commendable motives in educating our sons to be able to sing in worship and the wonderful academic bonuses they extraneously received, nothing is as important as that they bring a "sacrifice of praise to God, that is, the fruit of [their] lips, giving thanks to His name" (Hebrews 13:15).

Shod With the Preparation of the Gospel

1. How has popular music in the secular world changed in your lifetime?
2. How has secular "gospel music" changed in your lifetime?
3. How have these changes affected some Christians and the music they sing in worship?
4. Is four-part harmony important to pass on to the next generation for singing in worship? Why or why not? (Research the changes in the style and type of vocal music used in worship since the first century.)
5. How important is the quality of singing in worship? Name some ways that singing in worship can be improved in the congregation where you attend.
6. How have we perhaps discouraged some individuals from participating in singing in worship? Is it a sin not to sing?
7. Is it possible to separate the singing of music with religious content for entertainment from the singing of religious music in worship? Is it ever appropriate for a Christian to sing religious music with an instrument?

Conclusion

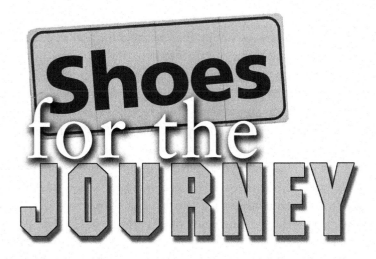

The butterfly days of my youth ended when I was 15. Admittedly, although my parents were strict in my upbringing, I was spoiled beyond measure. I had more security in my life than perhaps any other child I knew. More than likely, I would not have written this book had my life continued in its carefree way. The writer of Hebrews reminds us, "For whom the Lord loves He chastens, And scourges every son whom He receives" (12:6). He surely loved my parents and me because He most certainly disciplined us.

In the summer of my 15th year, I was scheduled to attend five different weeks of camps, including band and choral camps, a journalism workshop at the University of Tennessee, 4-H district camp, and state 4-H Roundup. On the way to band camp at Austin Peay State University on a Sunday afternoon in August, we were in a horrific automobile accident. My dad's brakes failed, and we were struck by an oncoming vehicle from the side. I spent one week in Vanderbilt Hospital in Nashville, Tenn. My mother was there for five weeks, and my dad stayed for 10 weeks, followed by multiple return weeks of operations and therapy. He was confined to a wheelchair for the rest of his life, and my mother, who was dependent upon him, became dependent upon me. After all, she could not even drive an automobile.

My junior year of high school was spent hearing my dad scream in pain during the night as my mother weaned him off codeine and Demerol. I drove the family car before I was the legal age, thanks to the local patrol who turned a blind eye. I shopped for groceries, bought medicine at the pharmacy, and banked for the family. All the chickens were sold, and in the summers I worked in our general merchandise store. After Daddy's health improved, my after-school hours were spent driving him and Mother, as well as my grandfather, through the countryside on pleasure trips because their lives were so confined.

Daddy gradually improved, and a few years later he was able to drive for short trips locally carrying his wheelchair with him behind the front seat. He read his Bible through multiple times; he said God had slowed him down for a purpose. When my mother died, he became very independent, even tending a garden from a golf cart and serving as a charter city commissioner in the newly incorporated Ethridge.

I grew up in a hurry in those days. The restraints my parents had used in training me in my earlier years helped me to be self-disciplined in the responsibilities so suddenly thrust upon me. I felt like I walked uphill both ways in my last two years of high school, but the trip made me who I am today, able to face the little hills and tall mountains along life's way.

In closing, I share with you a poem written when I was an 18-year-old sophomore in college, just as I was recovering from three years of what I now recognize as depression from this life-altering event. Although the poem may lack literary value, its philosophy is one I live by even today.

The Journey of Life

I started out on my journey through life
With faith and hope and my trust in God,
Knowing that people would taunt, "You can't."
My answer was ready, "I can! I can!"

Day after day I climbed the slope,
I reached, I struggled, I fought, I prayed;
And all the time they cried, "You can't!",
I merely replied, "I can! I can!"

Sometimes I slipped and lost my gains,
But I never lost hope, and I never lost faith;
And still they cried, "You can't! You can't!"
I answered calmly, "I will. I will."

Just when the top was close in view,
Just when my struggle was almost through,
They cried for the last time, "No, you'll fail!"
But I replied, "I can and I will!"

Now I stand and gaze from the top,
Watching others struggle up the road,
And I give them my secret – faith in God,
For He and I, we could and we did!

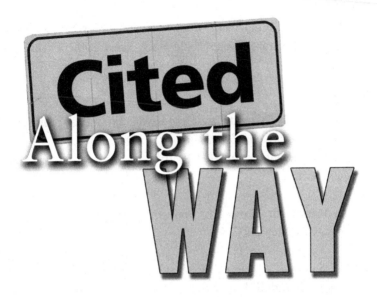

Chapter 1

Bentley, John. "The Problem of Internet Pornography." PowerPoint presentation. Freed-Hardeman U, Henderson, TN, Jan. 2006.

"Henley, William Ernest." *The Columbia Encyclopedia*. 6th ed. (2007). *Bartleby.com: Great Books Online*. 2008. 20 May 2007 <http://www.bartleby.com/65/he/Henley-W.html>.

"Pastors Viewing Internet Pornography." Survey. *Leadership* Winter 2001: 89.

"Temperance." Def. 1. *Webster's Revised Unabridged Dictionary (1913). DICT.org*. 2005. 27 May 2008 <http://www.dict.org/bin/Dict>.

"Tempt." Def. 1.Webster's *Third New International Dictionary*. Unabridged. 1981.

Chapter 2

Frost, Robert. "Mending Wall." *Early Frost: The First Three Books.*
Ed. Jeffrey Meyers. Edison: Castle-Book Sales, 1999. 47-48.

Chapter 3

Amadeo, Kimberly. "Credit Card Debt Up 8% From Last Year." 26
Oct. 2007. *About.Com: U.S. Economy.* 17 Dec. 2007
<useconomy.about.com/b/2007/10/26/credit-card-debt-up-8-from-last-year.htm>.

Baptiste, Mary Beth. "Love on a Shoestring: Our $150 Wedding."
Newsweek 21 May 2007: 14.

"Money." *Swindoll's Ultimate Book of Illustrations and Quotes.* Ed.
Charles R. Swindoll. Nashville: Nelson, 1998. 388-94.

Pullias, Athens Clay. "A.M. Burton: 'A Prince and a Great Man.' "
Gospel Advocate (27 Oct. 1966): 673, 679, 680. *The Restoration
Movement.* 2000. 17 June 2007 <www.therestoration
movement.com/burton,am.htm>.

Steinriede, Kent. "Those Little, Daily Things Wreak Big Budget
Havoc." *Tennessean* 31 March 2005: E1-2.

Chapter 4

"Gifts." *The Tale of the Tardy Oxcart.* Ed. Charles R. Swindoll.
Nashville: Word-Nelson, 1998. 229-230.

Chapter 5

In the Womb: Multiples. Documentary. National Geographic. 2006.
DVD, 2007.

Povich, Elaine S. "Her House." *AARP Bulletin* Jan. 2007: 30-31.

• **For Further Study**
Many periodicals today have excellent articles that give specific suggestions for dealing with sibling rivalry. These articles can be found reprinted in online databases such as *WilsonWeb* or *Gale Group*, available through a school or local library. Here are a few:
Barbour, Celia. " 'That's Not Fair!': Why You Can't Always Be Evenhanded (And Why You Don't Have to Try)." *Parenting* 1 Apr. 2006: 64.
McLaurin, Jennie A. "Foe ... or Friend? How to Rein in Sibling Rivalry." *Christian Parenting Today* Wtr. 2004: 40-.
"Tips for Taming Sibling Rivalry." *Jet* 28 June 2004: 22-.

Chapter 6
Bryant, William Cullen. "Thanatopsis." *The Norton Anthology of American Literature*. Ed. Gottesman et al. New York: Norton, 1979. Vol. 1 of 2. 673-75.

"Death." *Swindoll's Ultimate Book of Illustrations and Quotes*. Ed. Charles R. Swindoll. Nashville: Nelson, 1998. 135-45.

Shakespeare, William. *Hamlet. The Complete Works of Shakespeare Third Edition*. Ed. David Bevington, Glenview, IL: Scott, Foresman and Company, 1980, 1094.

Chapter 7
Brus, Brian. "Public Enemy #13." *Journal Record (Oklahoma City, OK)* 13 Apr. 2007: N. pag. *InfoTrac OneFile*. Gale. Loretto High School Lib., Loretto, TN. 10 June 2007 <http://infotrac.galegroup.com/itk12/tel_k_loretto>.

Emerson, Ralph Waldo. "Luck." *WorldofQuotes.com*. Ed. Roy Russo. 2003-2006. 27 Dec. 2007 <www.worldofquotes.com/author/ Ralph-Waldo-Emerson/5/index.html>.

Ingersoll, Robert Green. *Superstition*. *Infidels.org*. 6 June 2007 <www.infidels.org/library/historical/robert_ingersoll/superstition. html>

Pink, Daniel H. "How to Make Your Own Luck." *Fast Company.com* June 2003: 78-. 5 June 2007 <www.fastcompany.com/ magazine/72/realitycheck.html>.

Richmond, Raymond Lloyd. A Guide to Psychology and Its Practice. 15 Feb. 2008. 31 May 2008 <www.guidetopsychology. com/dreams.htm>.

Shakespeare, William. *Hamlet. The Complete Works of Shakespeare* Third Edition. Ed. David Bevington, Glenview, IL: Scott, Foresman and Company, 1980, 1085.

"Superstition." Def. 1. *The American Heritage Dictionary of the English Language*. New College Edition, 1976.

Wilhelm, Joseph. "Superstition." *The Catholic Encyclopedia*. Vol. 14. New York: Robert Appleton Company, 1912. 7 June 2007 <http://www.newadvent.org/cathen/14339a.htm>.

• For Further Study

I recommend two books that teach about death. The first is an excellent discussion of biblical teachings on life after death. The second is a personal story of loss and is helpful to those who are suffering from the death of a loved one.

Lyon, Mack. *Life, Death, and Beyond*. Huntsville, AL: Publishing Designs, 1994.

Scott, Pat. *Batten Down the Hatches*. Nashville: 21st Century, 1997.

Chapter 8

Frieden, Joyce. "Bullied Children More Prone to Depression: Raises Suicide Risk." *Family Practice News* 1 Jan. 2004: 79. *InfoTrac OneFile*. Gale. Loretto High School Lib., Loretto, TN. 10 June 2007 <http://infotrac.galegroup.com/itk12/tel_k_loretto>.

"Is 'Masculinity' Behind School Shooting?" *USA Today Magazine*
May 2005: 7. *InfoTrac OneFile*. Gale. Loretto High School Lib.,
Loretto, TN. 10 June 2007
<http://infotrac.galegroup.com/itk12/tel_k_loretto>.

"Mom Indicted in Deadly MySpace Hoax" Associated Press, 15
May 2008. CNN.com. 31 May 2008 <http://www.cnn.com/2008/
CRIME/05/15/internet.suicide.ap>.

Piazza, Peter. "Scourge of the Schoolyard." *Security Management*
Nov. 2001: 68-. *InfoTrac OneFile*. Gale. Loretto High School Lib.,
Loretto, TN. 10 June 2007 <http://infotrac.galegroup.com/itk12/
tel_k_loretto>.

Reist, Michael. "Unspoken Truth About Bullying." *Catholic New
Times* 23 Apr. 2006: 31-3. *InfoTrac OneFile*. Gale. Loretto High
School Lib., Loretto, TN. 10 June 2007 <http://infotrac.gale-
group.com/itk12/tel_k_loretto>.

Smith-Heavenrich, Sue. "Kids Hurting Kids: Bullies in the
Schoolyard." *Mothering* May-June 2001: 70. *InfoTrac OneFile*.
Gale. Loretto High School Lib., Loretto, TN. 10 June 2007
<http://infotrac.galegroup.com/itk12/tel_k_loretto>.

Woody, Larry. "Harvick Drives Way to a Checkered Win."
Tennessean 19 Feb. 2007: 1C+.

Yandrick, Rudy M. "Lurking in the Shadows." *HRMagazine* Oct
1999: 60-. *Human Resources Management. InfoTrac OneFile*.
Gale. Loretto High School Lib., Loretto, TN. 10 June 2007
<http://infotrac.galegroup.com/itk12/tel_k_loretto>.

Chapter 9

Baker, K.C. "You Can't Live Here … (Unless You're White)." *Good Housekeeping* 1 Apr. 2007: 174-. *InfoTrac OneFile*. Gale. Loretto High School Lib., Loretto, TN. 10 June 2007 <http://infotrac. galegroup.com/itk12/tel_k_loretto>.

"Prejudice." Def. 1a. *The American Heritage Dictionary of the English Language*. New College Edition, 1976.

"Racism." Dictionary.com Unabridged (v 1.1). Random House, Inc. 22 June 2007. *Dictionary.com* <http://dictionary.reference.com/ browse/racism>.

"Sexism." Def. 1 and 2. *The American Heritage Dictionary of the English Language*. New College Edition, 1976.

"Xenophobia." *The New Dictionary of Cultural Literacy*. 3rd ed. Houghton Mifflin, 2002. Bartleby.com. 10 June 2008 <www.bartleby.com/59/17/xenophobia.html>.

Chapter 10

Lincoln, Abraham. quoted in *The Columbia Book of World Quotations*. New York: Columbia University Press, 1996. Bartleby.com. 3 Oct. 2007 <http://www.bartleby.com/ 66/95/36395.html>.

Parkinson, C. Northcote. quoted in *The Columbia Book of World Quotations*. New York: Columbia University Press, 1996. Bartleby.com. 3 Oct. 2007 <http://www.bartleby.com/ 66/29/43629.html>.

Piercy, Marge. "To Be of Use." *American Poems … Your Poetry Site*. Gunnar Bengtsson. 2000-07. 4 Oct. 2007 <http://www.american poems.com/poets/Marge-Piercy/17193>.

"Prayer." *The Tale of the Tardy Oxcart*. Ed. Charles R. Swindoll. Nashville: Word-Nelson, 1998. 450-56.

Shakespeare, William. *Henry V. The Complete Works of Shakespeare* Third Edition. Ed. David Bevington, Glenview, IL: Scott, Foresman and Company, 1980, 878.

Chapter 11

Anderson, Kay. "The Consumer Counts: The Pampering of Our Pets." *Home Accents Today* Sept. 2003: 58-60. Findarticles.com 4 October 2007 <http://findarticles.com>.

"Animals of the Bible." *Nelson's New Illustrated Bible Dictionary*. Ed. Ronald F. Youngblood. Nashville: Nelson, 1995.

Cobas, Michelle. "USF Study Finds Childhood Animal Cruelty Is Indicator for Violent Offenders." USF: University of South Florida. News Archives. 1 Mar. 2003. 7 October 2007 <http://usfnews.usf.edu/page.cfm?link=article&aid=358>.

Ferguson, Everett. "Wine as a Table-Drink in the Ancient World." *Restoration Quarterly* (13:3) 1970: 141-153.

Chapter 12

Chesser, Frank. *Portrait of God*. Huntsville, AL: Publishing Designs, 2004.

Price, John. *Old Light on New Worship*. Avinger, TX: Simpson, 2005.

Wilhelm, Jack. *Smile, Seriously!* Florence, AL: Cox Creek, 1982.

• **For Further Study**

Some excellent studies of worship practices are available. I recommend the following:

Guy, Cynthia Dianne. *What About the Women?* Nashville: Gospel Advocate, 2005.

We Bow Down: Women Look at Worship. Huntsville, AL: Publishing Designs, 2002.

Chapter 13

"The Biology of Music." *Economist* (US) 12 Feb. 2000: 83. *InfoTrac OneFile.* Gale. Loretto High School Lib., Loretto, TN. 10 Nov. 2007 <http://infotrac.galegroup.com/itk12/tel_k_loretto>.

Congreve, William. *The Columbia Book of World Quotations.* New York: Columbia University Press, 1996. Bartleby.com. 27 Dec. 2007 <http://www.bartleby.com/66/87/13087.html>.

Gill, Chris, Jame Rotondi, and Jas Obrecht. "Within You Without You: The Guitarist's Search for Spiritual Meaning." *Guitar Player* May 1995: 48-. *InfoTrac OneFile.* Gale. Loretto High School Lib., Loretto, TN. 10 Nov. 2007 <http://infotrac.galegroup.com/itk12/tel_k_loretto>.

Jennings, Ralph. "With Some Discordant Notes Here and There, Area Hospitals Use Soothing Powers of Music." *The Business Journal* 10 Oct. 1994: 28-. *InfoTrac OneFile.* Gale. Loretto High School Lib., Loretto, TN. 10 Nov. 2007 <http://infotrac.galegroup.com/itk12/tel_k_loretto>.

"Music on the Brain: Experts Still Don't Know How or Why Tunes Tickle Our Fancy – But New Research Offers Intriguing Clues." *Time* 5 June 2000: 74-. *InfoTrac OneFile.* Gale. Loretto High School Lib., Loretto, TN. 10 Nov. 2007 <http://infotrac.gale group.com/itk12/tel_k_loretto>.

Price, John. *Old Light on New Worship.* Avinger, TX: Simpson, 2005.

Sousa, David A. "How the Arts Develop the Young Brain: Neuroscience Research Is Revealing the Impressive Impact of Arts Instruction on Students' Cognitive, Social and Emotional Development." *School Administrator* Dec. 2006: 26-. *InfoTrac OneFile*. Gale. Loretto High School Lib., Loretto, TN. 10 Nov. 2007 <http://infotrac.galegroup.com/itk12/tel_k_loretto>.

Prejudice:
Segregation in Churches
Xenophobia Racism distrust of other cultures
Matt 5:44
Luk 23:34 Jesus forgave his executeners
Matt 28:19-20

Joseph
Moses
Esther
Semantan woman
Egyptian Eunuch
Ruth

CPSIA information can be obtained
at www.ICGtesting.com
Printed in the USA
LVOW01s2013011115

460629LV00001B/4/P